Dr. JANET JONES

SOCIOLOGY IN ACTION

INVESTIGATING DEVIANCE

STEPHEN MOORE

UNWIN HYMAN

Published in 1988 by
Unwin Hyman Limited
15/17 Broadwick Street
London W1V 1FP

Reprinted 1990

British Library Cataloguing in Publication Data

Moore, Stephen
    Investigating deviance.–
    (Sociology in action series)
    1. Deviance – Sociological perspectives
    I. Title   II. Series
    302.542

    ISBN 0–7135–2837–0

Cover by Oxford Illustrators
Designed by Bob Wright
Cartoons by Shaun Williams

Typeset by August Filmsetting, Haydock, St Helens
Printed in Great Britain by Butler & Tanner Ltd, Frome, Somerset

Contents

Introduction

The *Sociology in Action* series aims to provide readers with an interesting and up-to-date account of the main themes in the areas covered. The series has been written primarily for students following the Sociology A Level and AS syllabus, and it is also designed to be helpful to those entering for examinations in related disciplines. The series will also prove valuable for those preparing for the Certificate Qualification in Social Work and Certificate of Social Studies examinations and for undergraduates following Sociology subsidiary courses. To this end, each book relates the issues specific to its subject area to the broader concerns of social science and the humanities. The philosophy underlying the series has been to encourage students to deepen their understanding of the subject by engaging in short exercises and larger-scale projects as they progress through the books. The authors have followed the student-centred approach which provided the impetus for the establishment of the GCSE syllabuses and AS Sociology for 1991.

In addition to A Level and AS Sociology, *Investigating Deviance* is also suitable for students following a wide range of professional and undergraduate courses where deviance occurs as a topic. *Investigating Deviance* was written because many topically important areas of the debate are ignored in textbooks currently available. In particular, crime in relationship to women and ethnic minorities has been given little coverage. Chapters 7 and 8 provide a full discussion of the relationship of women to crime, both as perpetrators, and as victims of crime. The debate about ethnic minorities and crime has been generally glossed over in other books. Chapter 9 considers this area in detail.

The other chapters of the book provide a firm grounding in all the topic areas required by the A Level and AS syllabuses. It is hoped that a degree of freshness, clarity and depth has been brought to these more traditional topics. Students are encouraged to conduct some small scale research projects, with the aim of making the study of Sociology an activity, rather than a passive process of reading or listening to a lecturer. I should emphasise that, in conducting their own research, students will develop a healthy cynicism of the research methods used by the sociologists mentioned in the main text.

Stephen Moore

Theoretical traditions in criminology

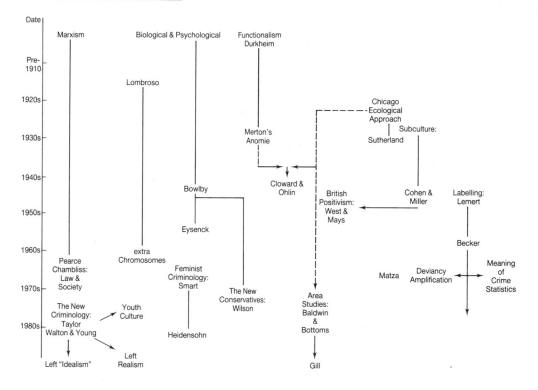

This book explores the contributions sociologists have made to the study of crime and deviance. Each chapter represents the different theoretical approaches that jostle with each other to offer their competing theories in the sociological marketplace. Within each of these chapters, certain issues which illustrate the theoretical perspective are studied and examined with a critical eye. The issues, such as delinquency, white-collar crime, marital violence or football hooliganism, are viewed primarily from the theoretical perspective that first raised the issues, but other contributions to that area are also included.

The major sociological approaches to crime and deviance in sociology are:

functionalism
ecology and subculture
labelling theory
Marxism
feminism
the New Right

Each of these has a chapter of its own in which the very significant differences between the approaches are drawn out. However, there are also major debates within sociology on two further issues: race and crime, and the nature of criminal statistics.

Before diving into the book, perhaps we can splash around in the shallows for a couple of pages and look briefly at some of the issues raised by these different perspectives. Firstly, an explanation of why chapters on race and crime, and the nature of criminal statistics, are included.

Race and crime; This has become a major issue to sociologists, mainly because there is a very bitter dispute indeed concerning the extent to which young blacks are disproportionately involved in minor street crime. Evidence from the Metropolitan Police to the Scarman Commission on the 1981 riots suggested that young blacks were posing a particular problem to law and order in London. The response from many was that the police were simply being racist, and they pointed to the damning evidence from the study of the Metropolitan Police in the early 1980s carried out by the research organisation PSI, which showed that racism was endemic amongst lower ranks. Yet, since then, a far more wide-ranging response has emerged which really reflects the state of contemporary sociological debate.

The nature of criminal statistics; At the time of writing, the Metropolitan Police have just released the 1987 criminal statistics for London. For the first time in at least twenty years, the crime rate has fallen. At first, this appears to be excellent news, yet many sociologists would argue that the crime statistics tell us more about the way that the police process the reports of crime given to them than any reflection of 'reality'. As we shall see in this chapter, the extent of crime in Britain seems to bear virtually no relationship to the official statistics. Yet, it is on these official statistics that most police and government policies are based.

Let us now turn to a brief examination of the theoretical approaches which form its main substance. Probably the simplest way of showing just how different all these approaches are, is to examine the different definitions of crime and deviance. In doing so, we will also see that there are important implications for research methods.

It helps to divide the various theoretical approaches into two general 'schools of thought' concerning the nature of deviance and its relationship to crime. The first 'school' can be called *the common-sense approach*, because it is the one most commonly used in ordinary discussion on crime. This approach is favoured by: functionalists, the New Right and less unanimously by subcultural theorists. The second school of thought can be called the *'relativist' approach* because it stresses the wide variations in what is defined as criminal or deviant. It is adhered to by labelling theorists, Marxist, and feminists.

Many different conceptions of right and wrong co-exist in British society, and those systems of rules can (be in) conflict. The law is different for the public and private sectors. There may be nothing legally wrong in a company manager behaving in a way which could lead to criminal charges against a public official. Also, officials may develop informal rules very different from those spelled out in the law and citizens will develop rules of their own out of everyday experiences within circles of co-workers and acquaintances.

In this chapter, we examine the results from a section of our questionnaire intended to establish how people judged a series of situations. From people's answers on the rightness and wrongness of these situations, we can try to identify some of the considerations people take into account and some of the rules they employ in judging social behaviour.

Popular conceptions of right and wrong are important because the law itself is often vague and thus, popular conceptions of right and wrong were critical in filling in the gaps of the law (Chibnall and Saunders, 1977).

Fiddling and the black economy have long been a fact of life. Whether or not people fiddle depends, in part, no doubt, upon whether or not they see it as wrong. An understanding of how people view the ethical aspects of everyday situations is a first step towards understanding the black economy from the inside out.

We are, in short, concerned with one of the basic problems in the relationship between state and society—the extent to which official rules agree with, or differ from, popular conceptions of right and wrong.

Source: Jowell and Witherspoon, *British Social Attitudes*, Gower, 1985

In order to illustrate these ideas of the variability of attitudes to right and wrong, Jowell and Witherspoon asked their respondents how they would judge the following situations:

'A householder is having a repair job done by a local plumber. He is told that if he pays cash he will not be charged VAT. So he pays cash.'

'A man offers the dustmen £5 to take away rubbish they are not supposed to pick up.'

'A man gives a £5 note for goods he is buying in a big store. By mistake, he is given change for a £10 note. He notices but keeps the change.'

The results of the judgements were:

	Evading VAT %	Bribing dustmen %	Pocketing wrong change %
Nothing wrong in it	31	32	6
A bit wrong	31	35	15
Wrong	32	29	61
Seriously wrong	3	3	16
Don't know	3	2	1

Asked if they would do it, the respondents replied:

	Evade VAT %	Bribe dustmen %	Pocket change %
I might do it	66	58	18
Don't know/no answer	7	4	5
I would not do it	27	38	77

Source: Jowell and Witherspoon, *British Social Attitudes* Gower, 1985

1 **What does the extract by Jowell and Witherspoon tell us concerning the nature of right and wrong?**
2 **Does the extract by Jowell and Witherspoon tell us anything about the nature of: a) deviance and b) law?**
3 **What does the first table tell us concerning attitudes to VAT, bribing dustmen, and pocketing the wrong change?**
4 **What does the second table tell us concerning the fit between people's attitudes and their actions? Does this have any implications for the meaning of 'deviant' and 'criminal'?**

PROJECT

Using the same model of research as above, devise a set of values and a questionnaire to check the validity of this study.

The common-sense view
The functionalist and New Right approaches

According to this perspective, society is characterised by basic agreement on the fundamental values that underpin our society. We all agree, for example, that helping others is good and hurting others is bad—so where is the problem?

Deviant behaviour is a form of behaviour which is in some way 'abnormal'. Arising from this definition is the distinction between deviant behaviour which is regarded as good, and that which is bad. Good behaviour may be deviant because so few people would have the courage to do it, such as the actions of Terry Waite, kidnapped in the Lebanon for his pains. How many ordinary people would run the risk of death and kidnap in order to obtain the freedom of people not even personally known to them? But deviant behaviour is most commonly thought of as being bad or evil, for example, inflicting pain on others. This simple, uncomplicated definition is one adopted by most people in their common-sense understanding of the world; armed with it we go about our daily lives, striving to be good (and admiring the very good) and sometimes, unfortunately, falling into bad (or deviant) behaviour. A third form of deviant behaviour is that which is 'odd' or bizarre. I am thinking here mainly of people suffering from some form of mental illness, which makes their behaviour unpredictable to the rest of us. These sorts of people cannot be defined as 'bad', but we do treat them differently and we keep ourselves well away from them.

Deviants and normal people

Deriving from this common definition of deviance is an important belief which most police officers, magistrates, social workers and all others who process the deviants of this world believe. This is that deviants are in some way *different* from the rest of us normal, rule-following types. Of course, by mistake a 'normal' person may commit the isolated deviant act, but the real deviant is one who consistently proves him/herself to be different from the rest of us.

The difference between illegal and deviant

Why is it that some deviant acts are legal—for example, 'odd' forms of sexual activity—yet other types of deviant acts are illegal? There is a common-sense answer to this, too. The further an act deviates from usual standards, particularly if it involves harm to others, the more likely it is to be made illegal. In particular, laws are passed because there is a common belief that certain actions are quite simply wrong and ought to be outlawed. In a democracy the laws will, therefore, reflect the views of the majority of people in society.

The implications for methodology

Functionalist and writers of the New Right have tended not to engage in much detailed research. Functionalists, like Marxists, have placed greater stress on abstract theorising.

The New Right has had considerable influence on the funding of official Home Office surveys which are concerned with collecting the 'facts' of crime. Typically, these are detailed studies of the relationship between policing or prison costs and the extent to which they deter crime. However, large numbers of studies are conducted from an apparently 'atheoretical' viewpoint. For example, the researcher may be interested in marital violence. Without any particular theory in mind, the researcher then looks at violent husbands and tries to find out anything unusual in their backgrounds or marriages (or even in the behaviour of the assaulted wife). These differences from the normal husband are then taken to be the *causes* of the violence. Most sociologists would argue that this form of *positivist* research, falls within the general range of the functionalist approach and tacitly makes the same assumptions. So, in reading research that purports to examine only 'the facts', without any theoretical bias, beware: almost certainly there is a hidden (usually functionalist) theory underlying it.

The ecological and subcultural approaches

What is deviant behaviour?

These approaches combine such a wide variety of ideas and methods that it is difficult to give a short summary.

Deviant behaviour is seen as forms of behaviour which certain groups engage in and which are different from the dominant ones of society. However, most subcultural theories recognise that in any society at one time there are a variety of different sets of values, according to which people measure their behaviour. Nevertheless, most subcultural and ecological theories accept that the mainstream 'dominant' values are the 'true' values of the majority of the population and deviance is the result of following subcultural values.

Deviants and 'normal' people

Deviants are seen as different from 'normal' people in that they follow quite distinctive sets of values from the majority. There is nothing 'wrong' with deviants, they merely subscribe to different values and, therefore, behave differently.

The differences between illegal and deviant acts

The functionalist argument by which the laws reflect the views of the majority are accepted, by most subcultural theories.

Implications for methodology

Subcultural and ecological theories stress that we need to understand the meanings which people give to their actions within the subcultures, therefore most subcultural and ecological theories have used *participant observation* which involves joining a group of people and trying to see the world through their eyes.

Some problems facing the 'common-sense' approach

The argument presented above remains unquestioned in most people's minds, but it requires a close analysis. At the time of writing, a Bill is being debated in Parliament concerning a reduction of the time limit for having a legal abortion—the Alton Bill (named after the Liberal MP who sponsored it). In effect, the Bill, if passed, will make certain abortions illegal. It could be argued that this Bill is being debated because it reflects the popular will—yet we know that the British population is divided on this issue. There is no 'consensus' or general agreement. The moral, medical and social arguments put forward are bitterly contested. No matter what the outcome of the Bill, the final law will not necessarily reflect the will of the people. The belief in some form of general agreement on acceptable behaviour is very dubious indeed; society does *not* consist of one set of homogenous, agreed values but a bewildering variety of viewpoints and beliefs.

Furthermore, we need to consider whether what people say they believe in really reflects their own opinions. Opinion polls regularly show that people would prefer to pay higher levels of income tax in order to eliminate poverty, provide good social services and maintain a decent National Health Service, yet on entering the polling booths the electorate over the last two elections have chosen a political party—the Conservatives—which places income tax cuts above all these things on its agenda. The search for a consensus of values seems to become even more elusive. Another problem for the common-sense approach is the way that the definition of 'deviant' varies across a remarkable range of factors, including time. For example, the way Victorian women were expected to behave was completely different from that expected today. For a literary exposition of this, see John Fowles' novel *The French Lieutenant's Woman*. It could be argued that the heroine of the book has sexual needs and a desire for self-fulfilment accepted as normal today, but is living in a society which regards them as disgusting and deviant. What causes the change in values concerning what is deviant?

A second example concerns *who* commits the act; for instance, theft through tax evasion is usually 'punished' by a rude letter and possibly the demand for a proportion of the underpayment to be paid to the Inland Revenue. On the other hand, theft of relatively worthless goods from a shop is often rewarded with a prison sentence.

More complications arise. Some more radical sociologists argue that the police and the judiciary are more likely to treat blacks harshly and yet others that females are treated more leniently!

For the time being, let us accept that the common-sense view is certainly not accepted by most sociologists. Instead, they point to a different approach to crime and deviance.

Relativist approaches to crime and deviance

The relativist approach to defining deviance and crime is provided by:

labelling theorists
Marxist approaches
feminist approaches.

Labelling theory

What is deviant behaviour?

The stress of the labelling approach is on the fact that what is defined as deviant varies widely according to a number of factors, including time, person, and place. Deviance cannot be defined in terms of particular acts, but rather in terms of how certain acts are defined by people in particular circumstances. For example, killing another person can be both deviant and heroic, legal and illegal, depending upon the circumstance. I am sure you can provide examples of situations in which this is so. There is no fixed definition of deviance, therefore, according to these writers, rather acts and people are defined as deviant according to the circumstances and the type of person who commits the act. This argument is followed in some detail on pages 55–57.

Deviants and normal people

Deviants, according to this view, are little different from non-deviants. It is not true to say there is a separate class of people who commit crimes because they are motivated by some special factor which distinguishes them from normal people. The distinction lies in the fact their behaviour is defined as deviant through the actions of other people.

The difference between deviant and illegal

Labelling theory argues that certain deviant behaviour becomes illegal as a result of pressure group activity (see pp. 57–59). A group of people band together to force through a change in the law to reflect their own interests or what they perceive to be the interests of the population in general. The Alton Bill described earlier is a good example of this.

The implications for methodology in the study of deviance

The labelling approach is not concerned at all to find the distinguishing features of deviants.
The most favoured approach to methods used by labelling theorists are:

a) *participant observation*; this method involves joining in with a group of labelled deviants and trying to understand the reasons why they act the way they do,
b) *content analysis*: this generally involves detailed examination of newspapers to follow the progress of a particular Bill, for example, in order to find out the dynamics of law making,
c) *case studies* of a particular group or legal occurrence are also popular. A case study involves following one particular event/place/group in detail.

Marxist approaches

What is deviant behaviour?

Marxist models of crime and deviance obviously develop from the basic Marxist concept of the exploitation of the working class (the proletariat) by the ruling class (the bourgeoisie). Deviant behaviour consists of activities which the ruling class define as wrong, immoral or illegal.

The consensus of values which underlies the common-sense approach is vehemently rejected here. Instead, society is seen as torn between the competing bourgeois and proletarian values. The power of the bourgeoisie and their ownership of the media play crucial roles in having their definitions of 'reality' accepted in society. However, there is always a threat to dominant values from the (socialist) values of the proletariat.

Deviants and normal people

The Marxist approach sees deviants as normal people. Usually, deviants consist of those groups the ruling class perceive as a threat to their power and stability, so they are persecuted. Much modern Marxism, for example, analyses the position of inner city youth. This is seen as a threat to capitalism, and hence the intense policing imposed on youth.

The *real* deviants are the ruling class who steal from, and exploit, the workers.

The difference between illegal and deviant

The difference between deviance and illegality is the degree to which they threaten the stability of the 'bourgeois state'.

More sophisticated Marxist analyses see a degree of complexity in this process and variations on the Marxist model stress that some laws are the result of working class pressure, for example.

The implications of this approach for methodology

Marxist approaches tend to be far more abstract than most other methods except for functionalism and there is possibly more theorising than actual studies. However, as the label 'Marxist' covers such a broad range of approaches, there are a number of different techniques used. In particular:

a) *participant observation* has been used in the study of delinquent groups of youths,

b) *case studies*, mainly using secondary information from newspapers, official investigations, etc, have been conducted to uncover white-collar and corporate crime,

c) in the last few years the Marxist-related approach *left realism* has begun to use *surveys* in order to uncover the way ordinary people feel about crime and what fears they have.

Feminist theory

Defining 'deviant' behaviour

The definition of deviant behaviour can be related to sexual inequality. It could be considered that the lives of women are controlled by man-made *mores* concerning how they ought to behave, so that women are not free, but closely controlled. It is very simple for a woman to be defined as deviant; they can be regarded as such simply by doing exactly the same things as men. For example, having a number of sexual partners or drinking alone in pubs are actions which are defined differently according to the sex of the person involved.

Deviants and normal people

Feminists believe that all women are controlled by men in some way or another. Women are likely to be defined as deviant when they engage in behaviour which is regarded as a rejection of their roles in society. They question the very idea of what is normal and centre their analysis on the construction of 'normality' (for women), by men.

The difference between illegal and deviant behaviour

One of the interesting facts which emerge from a study of crime and gender, is that relatively few women compared to men commit criminal acts. According to feminists, the crime of 'soliciting' is one which reflects the combination of the way sexuality is constructed in our society and the economic inequalities that exist. In a male-dominated society men are justified in seeking out sex, because it is claimed that men 'need' sex because of their (theoretically) greater sex drive. Women, according to feminists, are driven to prostitution through economic motives.

However, illegality is not the main issue for females. Rather the main issue is the social control placed on them and the definition of their role in such a way as to make 'normal male' behaviour deviant for them.

A final important point is that females encounter the law more as *victims* of particular crimes (rape and marital violence, for example), than as perpetrators of crimes.

☐ **Construct a table to summarise the differences between approaches in sociology. Use your own headings or the ones used in this chapter.**

The implications for methodology

There is not yet a 'body' of feminist studies of crime and deviance, although the field is a very active one. Feminists have tended to draw from a wide range of studies to prove their points concerning the social control of women:

a) *secondary sources*: official studies and sociological surveys have shown that women are discriminated against and 'repressed' in many areas of life. Feminists researching the area of female deviance have used this evidence in some detail,

b) *intensive case studies*: these have been used by feminist researchers, usually on groups of teenage girls in school, in order to find out more about their attitudes and behaviour.

☐ **ESSAYS**

1 **Compare and contrast the main theoretical perspectives used by sociologists in the study of deviance, illustrating your answer with examples.**

2 **Explain why different theoretical approaches tend to be associated with different methodological approaches. Illustrate your answer with examples.**

3 *All* **acts which are criminal are deviant.** *Some* **acts which are deviant are criminal. Some acts which are deviant are** *good.* **Explain and discuss these statements using relevant examples.**

Bibliography

If you wish to explore the issues of methodology further, undoubtedly the clearest introduction is Pat McNeill's *Research Methods*, Tavistock, 1985. Most introductory textbooks will cover sociological theory. The final chapter of *Teach Yourself Sociology* by S. Moore and B. Hendry (Hodder and Stoughton, 1982) gives a short, clear summary.

Feminist theory is explained in *Current trends in Feminist Theory* by Mary Maynard, *Social Studies Review*, January 1987.

2 · Functionalist Perspectives

The functionalist approach to crime

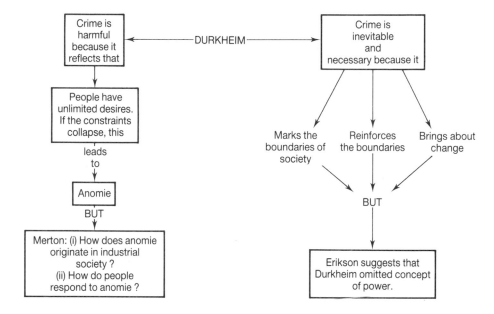

Functionalist explanations of crime

Functionalist explanations derive from the work of Emile Durkheim who was writing at the end of the last century.

According to Durkheim, there are two crucial elements in understanding crime, which at first sight appear to be contradictory. A *limited amount* of crime is necessary and beneficial to society, so much so that society could not exist without some form of deviance. On the other hand, *too much* crime is bad for society and can help to bring about its collapse.

So the *amount* of crime is the distinguishing feature between its being good or bad for society. This contrasts with the typical view that crime, by its very nature, is harmful to society.

The necessity of crime

Durkheim's view is that a society consists of common expectations regarding behaviour, based upon shared values and beliefs. We all agree what is right and wrong and act accordingly. However, the boundaries of acceptable behaviour need to be defined and made known to all. This is exactly the role of criminal law.

First, the law unambiguously marks the extremities of acceptable behaviour. Each time the police arrest a person, they are making it clear to the rest of society that that particular action is unacceptable. Second, the boundaries must be made known to everyone in society, so some form of publicity and drama needs to be generated. Erikson has pointed out, for example the dramatic setting of the courtroom where the lawyers and judges dress in special clothes, and where there is a ceremony which condemns a person's actions in a public arena. In contemporary society, newspapers help to perform this publicity function, with their often lurid accounts of criminal acts. In effect, the courts and the media are

□ **Durkheim suggests that crime is both inevitable in society and also necessary. In a society of 'saints' there would have to be 'crime', for without crime society would not exist.**

1 **How could there possibly be crime in a society of saints?**

2 **What common values do you think all of us share? How could you find these out in practice?**

3 **Some socialists believe that in a socialist society, without exploitation, there would be no crime. Do you believe that this is achievable?**

'broadcasting' the boundaries of acceptable behaviour, warning others not to breach the walls of the law (and, therefore, society).

A further function performed by criminals is to provide a constant test of the boundaries of permitted action. For example, every time that a person is prosecuted for a crime, attention is brought to the committal of that act. People can express their feelings about this—in most cases this is simply an unquestioning acceptance of the illegality and evil nature of the act. However, sometimes people may feel sympathy with the criminal. In this case the law is clearly out of step with the feelings and values of the majority and there is a need to reform the law. Criminals, therefore, provide a crucial service in helping the law to reflect the wishes of the population and legitimising social change.

A final element of Durkheim's model follows from this 'boundary-testing' function just described. When particularly horrific crimes are carried out, the result is to draw people together in feelings of mutual horror or fear (or both), so the bonds between them are strengthened.

The effect of crime on society

Durkheim was careful, however, to balance his arguments over the necessity of crime with its damaging effects on society if allowed to go unchecked. According to Durkheim and the functionalist tradition that followed him, society is based on a set of shared values which he calls the 'collective conscience'. It is not that people *naturally* hold this collective conscience, rather people are naturally self-seeking and wish to look after their own interests at the expense of others. What stops them is the law and the collective conscience, which is taught to all of us through the process of socialisation.

The law is, however, the weaker of the two enforcement agencies. Far stronger is the all pervasive 'self-control' operated by the collective conscience on all of us. However, in periods of great social strain or dramatic change, the power of the collective conscience is weakened. When Durkheim was writing, for example, there was great fear that the community life had been shattered by the growth of major cities and of industrialisation. As the community collapsed under the weight of the dramatic social change brought about by industrialisation and urbanisation, so the collective conscience was weakened. The result, according to Durkheim, was the development of a state he called *anomie*. In essence this means that people regard as unimportant the social expectations on them to respect the rights and needs of others and they prefer instead to look after their own interests, even at the expense of those of their neighbours. They return to their 'natural' state of greed and self-interest. For society this is the long-term collapse of order and harmony.

Anomie, then, is a harmful and dangerous state.

The contribution of Durkheim

Durkheim's writing represented a major breakthrough in understanding the nature of deviance. Most other late-nineteenth century writers on crime were trying to find out what was *wrong* with criminals and deviants. Durkheim argued that crime was not the result of some 'sick' individuals, nor was it in any way 'unnatural', rather deviance was an integral part of society which performed an absolutely crucial function.

However, there are a number of problems connected with the

Durkheim view. The first is that he offered no real explanation as to why certain people were more likely to commit deviant acts than others. He was not really concerned with this problem. Durkheim was really interested in the *nature* of the relationship between deviance and order in society. However, if questioned on the individual motivations of criminals, he would probably have stressed their lack of adequate socialisation.

A second problem lies in his stress on the harmony of society and the belief that the law reflects the interests and views of the majority of the population. He seems almost wilfully to ignore the concept of *power*. It is generally accepted that in all societies some groups have greater ability than the bulk of the population to influence the law making process.

So, although Durkheim led the way in relating crime and deviance to the very structure of society itself, he failed, first, to explain the reasons why some people commit crime and second, to explore the element of power in law making.

These two elements of Durkheim's writing have been extended—the positive aspect of deviance has led to the work of Erikson, while the negative aspect of deviance has been developed by Merton.

Erikson: the positive aspect of crime

In the mid–1960s Erikson developed Durkheim's ideas on the *boundary setting* and *maintainance* functions of crime. However, he made one particularly important alteration to Durkheim's original explanation. According to Durkheim, the collective conscience, and the laws that derived from it were a reflection of the will of the people. Erikson suggested that Durkheim had omitted the differences in *power* that exist in society. He, therefore, showed how crime set the boundaries of permissible action, but did so in the interests of the powerful. In doing so, he made a bridge between the functionalist and Marxist schools of thought.

In *Wayward Puritans*, Erikson explored how religious Puritan leaders imposed their rulings on their followers.

In the seventeenth century, the European Puritans began to emigrate to 'the New World' in order to escape persecution. This persecution was a result of the Puritan belief that God speaks directly to each person, without the need of any intermediary such as a church. Churches, however, played a central role in maintaining social order on behalf of the European States. They often conveniently interpreted God's will as a reflection of the views of their Governments. By preaching the irrelevance of the church the Puritans were undermining a major prop of government.

Within the Puritan communities, the leaders derived their authority from leading the opposition to oppression. After the flight to America, this basis for authority was removed—if God spoke directly to each person, then what role did leaders have? To give themselves a role, the old leadership began to alter the previously held beliefs. Yes, it was true that God spoke directly to individuals, but only a select few (the leadership) could correctly interpret what God said!

Many Puritans were unhappy about this and one, a certain Mrs Hutchinson, rebelled. She was brought to trial, acccused of witchcraft (she was listening to the devil not God), convicted and thrown out of the congregation.

The effect of the trial was that the new law was legitimised and the threat to the leadership was disgraced. Furthermore, the rest of the Puritans were drawn together in horror.

Strain theory: the work of Merton

Merton also used the concept of anomie. However, he regarded the idea as too vague in its original form and so altered it to mean a society where there is a 'disjunction between goals and means'. In such a society, there is, according to Merton, a tremendous cultural stress on being successful (the goal), and yet it is virtually impossible for the majority of the population ever to achieve success in a socially acceptable way (the means). In a situation like this, the burning desire to achieve the socially-stressed goals actively promotes deviant behaviour.

Merton was not simply putting forward an abstract argument, he was describing, as he saw it, the United States of the 1930s. According to him, American society had become almost obsessed with the desire to make money, indeed it was only the possession of this that indicated success in life. All other values and all other measures of success seemed to pall compared to the crucial ones of money and wealth.

However, Merton pointed to the fact that the vast bulk of the American population had little or no chance of legally ever becoming rich. For the struggling immigrants, the urban poor and the American blacks, the 'American dream' was just that—a dream.

This explanation follows Durkheim, and is 'structural' because Merton locates the cause of deviance in the very nature of United States' society itself, not in any defect that originates in the individual.

Merton did not suggest that everyone who was denied access to the very peaks of wealth entered the state of anomie, rather he argued that there were quite clear bands of expectations. Those who start at the bottom do not necessarily expect to get to the very top, but aspire to a prosperous standard of living. On the other hand, those from relatively affluent backgrounds seriously aspire to be rich.

Having laid out his general principal that being blocked from success leads to deviance, Merton then moved on to explain the fact that people choose *different* patterns of deviance: for example, one person may steal while another may take drugs.

Before we move on, examine the table below, which shows the various responses that Merton suggested may take place in a situation of anomie.

Responses	*Means*	*Goals*
Conformity	+	+
Innovation	−	+
Ritualism	+	−
Retreatism	−	−
Rebellion	±	±

Notes: + = acceptance of the goals or means.
 − = rejection of the goals or means.
 ± = rejection of the goals and means, and substitution of new ones.

Conformity: occurs when the person continues to accept the goals and the means set by society, even though 'failure' is the likely outcome. The typical law-abiding citizen.

Innovation: is the response when a person accepts the goals set by society,

☐ **PROJECT**

Merton's argument is based on the idea that people share similar values. Devise a series of questions which will indicate whether people hold, or do not hold, a range of values which you decide may be important. For example, a question concerning future career choice could indicate whether people were interested in making money alone. Ask a small sample of people. As a result of this would you agree with Merton that there are agreed goals that people are keen to obtain?

but rejects the socially-acceptable means. Here, people may turn to crime for financial rewards, or may simply find a new (legal) way of making money.

Ritualism: is where the means to the goals are accepted and conformed to, but the person loses sight of the goals. The person, therefore, 'goes through the motions' but has no real interest in the outcome. For example, the teacher who stresses the importance of neat handwriting, but ignores the contents of an essay.

Retreatism: in this response, both the goals and the means are lost sight of. The person simply 'drops out of the rat race', the typical responses would be drug abuse or alcoholism.

Rebellion: the last response is one where the person rejects the current society with its stress on success and also rejects the means that society provides to obtain the goals. In terms of the model, a rejection of both means and goals takes place, and alternative goals and means are substituted. Political radicals and terrorists are examples of this.

The model provides us with the *reason* why people deviate (anomie) and the *types* of deviance which people enter (rejection and acceptance of means/goals). Because it stresses that crime is the outcome of a strain between what people wish to achieve and what is possible, the theory is often known as *strain theory*.

Merton's explanation for deviance has been criticised by a number of sociologists: indeed, it has become a standard textbook criticism to suggest that Merton gives no explanation as to why a particular person chooses one form of deviance in preference to another. This is not true; Merton argues that different levels and types of ritualistic and innovative behaviour by social class is the reflection of the different emphases in socialisation between the middle and working classes.

According to Merton, the working class person, having been socialised in a less rigid way, can violate conventional expectations of behaviour with less guilt and anxiety. Socialisation channels people into various responses by limiting the choice of deviant adaptations open to people. This is not to say that Merton is in any way sympathetic to subcultural theory, rather he regards normal societies as those which agree on basic values and acceptable patterns of behaviour. It is just that the emphases on socialisation vary from one social group to another.

There is a money madness in the air which goes beyond the traditional American passion for the almighty buck. Like the steady drinker who one day slips into alcoholism, America has lost control of its greed.

Greed is fashionable, and restraint is out of style. Ivan Boesky, before his downfall, was a popular speaker at colleges, where he preached the undiluted gospel of naked avarice. Greed is driven by a fearful sense that there may not be much time. Slow accumulation, long-term strategy and forward planning are relics from an earlier age of innocence. The sense of economic doom which hangs over the country is almost palpable.

At a recent conference in Boston on 'The American Dream', not a single paper that I heard deviated from the convention that the dream has nothing to do with freedom or democracy, and everything to do with living standards. In the annual opinion poll of entering college students this academic year, 70 per cent gave as their reason for entering college 'to make more money,' and more than a quarter of all students were headed for business studies. Questioned about their essential goals in life, 73 per cent of new students chose 'being very well off financially'. Both these percentages have gone up by a third in the last ten years while the proportion of students who have ambitions to do 'something creative' with their lives has sunk to 10 per cent. On the wall of the men's room in the University library some young philosopher has summed up the *zeigeist*: 'Whoever dies with the most toys, wins.'

Source: Bouchier, 'The Great Greed of 1987', *The New Statesman*, 12 June, 1987

□ 1 Explain how *The New Statesman* extract relates to Merton.

2 According to Merton, anomie is a state which indicates that there is something temporarily wrong with capitalism, which can be cured by strengthening the other values in society besides greed. For Marxists, however, capitalism is all about greed and envy. Which of these descriptions of capitalism is more accurate?

3 As a result of your reply to the question above—what type of policy would you suggest for eradicating crime?

4 Merton has been criticised for ignoring the idea of power. What is meant by this?

5 Is it true that British society is 'anomic'? Devise a very simple questionnaire to evaluate the attitudes towards wealth and success of a group of: a) students; b) the general public.

Suicide

The study of suicide by Durkheim, and its subsequent criticisms by Atkinson and Douglas has by now become a classic example of methodological and theoretical changes in sociology. It illustrates the deep divisions in the subject between those who believe in following the methods of the natural sciences wherever possible—an approach known as *positivism*—and those who prefer to explore the realm of the construction of meanings by individuals—*subjective* or *phenomenological sociology*.

The background to the study

Suicide had fascinated researchers throughout the nineteenth century and there had been a great variety of explanations offered, including: insanity (organico-psychic dispositions as Durkheim phrased it!); geographical features such as climate, temperature and length of day; and finally, that suicide was the result of people imitating each other! It is worth remembering that all three of these explanations are still offered today, with phrases like suicide 'whilst the balance of mind was upset', or in newspaper discussions of 'copycat sucides'. Durkheim dismissed all of these

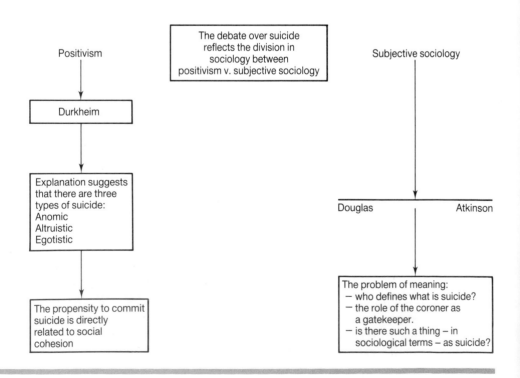

explanations by collecting statistics from a number of countries, and then tested them against each of the 'causes' mentioned above to show there was no relationship. However, he was influenced by the work of some statisticians who showed that suicide rates increased in times of social change and that they varied according to religious groups. These ideas fitted in with his theories concerning *social integration* which we shall examine shortly.

Durkheim had chosen suicide to prove the usefulness of sociology in explaining social phenomena, at a time when the subject was not taken seriously as an academic discipline. If he could prove that one of the most *individual* acts any human being could perform, that is killing him/herself, could be explained through social factors, then surely *any* action could be examined in such a way. The method chosen by Durkheim, which I described above we now call *multi-variate analysis*, consisting of comparing the influence of various social factors on the incidence of a particular event (suicide). This was so well done by Durkheim that in textbooks seventy years later it was still being given as an excellent example of research methodology. We shall see later just how mistaken the writers of these textbooks were.

The theory

The starting-point for Durkheim was a close analysis of the available official statistics, which showed that rates of suicide varied:

   in different countries,
   in different regions within countries,
   by different social groups (eg, the married and unmarried),
   by different religious groups (Jews, Protestants, Catholics),

and that the rates were relatively stable over time for each of these groups, that is, they retained the different levels of suicide relative to each other over a twenty year period.

Now if suicide was an entirely individual matter untouched by the influence of social factors, it would be an astonishing coincidence if these statistical patterns remained so constant within each group or society, over a long period of time. Entirely individual decisions should lead to a random pattern, one would have thought.

Social integration

Durkheim's explanation centred on his concept of social cohesion and integration, which, as we saw earlier, underpins his analysis of crime. For Durkheim, people were not naturally social animals, mankind has to be constrained and 'bonded' to the values of society, otherwise individual greed and self-interest will take over. For him, societies were social organisations based upon common values that allowed people to co-operate with each other in harmony, as long as the individuals felt a common bond.

There were a number of ways in which people were 'bonded' to society, but the main means of *social integration*, as Durkheim called it, were the family and religion. Durkheim suggested that individuals who felt most closely tied to society were ones with close family relationships in particular, where there was a sense of commitment to others and, therefore, to society. Of course, this meant that those without close family (or similar) ties were least bonded to society.

Religion operated on a broader level, influencing the whole ethos of society by providing people with a moral underpinning of social rules. However, Durkheim argued that different religions placed different levels of stress on the relative importance of fulfilling *individual* satisfaction and interests. At the one extreme, Protestant religions placed considerable importance on the individual fulfilling him/herself, while religions such as Hinduism or Catholicism stressed far more the importance of the group and the relative unimportance of searching for personal happiness.

It is important to remember that religion was a far more powerful influence on social life in the last century than it is now, and directly affected the way individuals behaved.

The outcome of these various influences on social integration was that societies could be placed on a scale depending on the extent they stressed individual or group interests.

Durkheim defined suicide as 'death resulting directly or indirectly from a positive or negative act performed by the victim himself which he knows will produce this result'. A positive act would be taking an overdose, a negative act would be when a Hindu wife allowed herself to be burned to death according to the traditional (but now illegal) Indian custom of *'suttee'*.

It was Durkheim's hypothesis that suicide is directly related to the levels of social integration in a society or group within a society. Durkheim isolated four types of social structures which fell at different points along the line of social integration:

egoistic,
altruistic,
anomic,
and fatalistic.

Egoistic

Egoistic social structures are those in which individual rights, interests and welfare are heavily stressed and where allegiance to the wider group is weak. People are encouraged to look after themselves and those particularly close to them at the expense of the wider society. As a result of this, the social bonds are weak and there is a low level of social integration. This form of social structure is typical of modern western industrial societies, where the competitive pursuit of individual happiness is promoted as a central value. According to Durkheim, the Protestant religion has been a particularly strong influence on the development of this form of social structure, mainly because Protestant values stress individual decisions and responsibilities. Furthermore, success and happiness on earth were taken to be a sign that God was looking favourably upon a particular person. In this sort of environment, individual failure or unhappiness are adequate grounds for people to take their own lives.

Within the wider egoistic society, however, there are particular social institutions which do provide people with strong social bonds and partly counteract the wider egoistic values of society. These include:

The family, which stresses the importance of mutual obligations between members, and in particular the role of husband/father and wife/mother.
Other religions, such as Catholicism, which place far greater stress on the importance of an individual's responsibility to the wider church. There is an insistence too on the observance of clear-cut rules of the church,

1. **How does Durkheim actually measure levels of social integration?**
2. **What ways could you suggest of adequately measuring social intregration?**

which gives the individual a strong feeling of *belonging*. In the case of Jews, Durkheim pointed out the extremely strong community feeling and the way this was maintained through an experience of persecution. *Times of external oppression*, when a society, or group (like the Jews) are threatened from outside, will draw people together, strengthening social integration.

Durkheim concluded, therefore, that there are likely to be relatively high rates of suicide in societies with low levels of social integration, but that *within* those societies, individuals in institutions which provide greater levels of social integration are less likely to take their own lives. For example, married people are less likely to commit suicide than single people.

Altruistic social structures

The opposite of egoistic societies are altruistic ones. Here, the individual is completely subsumed into the group and views its existence as far more important than his/her own. Altruistic social structures exert an extremely powerful influence over the actions of the individuals, so that what the social structure dictates, the person will do. Durkheim described this form of society as having *insufficient individuation*.

In these forms of society, the suicide rate is much lower for individual reasons of unhappiness. Instead those suicides which occur tend to be ones which are demanded by the culture of the social structure, and the individual accepts death as the only possible action. The example I gave earlier of the Hindu practice of *'suttee'* is the one used by Durkheim himself, where the widow sacrifices herself on her husband's funeral pyre.

Soldiers too, and in particular officers, are more likely to sacrifice their lives for the good of the army than an ordinary individual would do. Durkheim explains this by claiming that a soldier 'must be drilled to set little value on his person'.

Anomic suicide

The third social situation which is related to the level of suicide is that of *anomie*. We discussed the concept of anomie earlier, so you will recall that Durkheim believed people were naturally greedy and self-interested, and only if they were restricted in their desires by controls placed on them by society could they actually live in harmony together. Going beyond this, Durkheim argued that people learned to measure their wants and desires by the norms or guidelines given them by society. If the social constraints were removed then people would feel lost and bewildered as they would have no standards to measure their behaviour against. In periods of rapid economic improvement, people would simply never be satisfied and the resultant disillusionment could lead to suicide. On the other hand, in periods of rapid economic decline, people might not be able to reconcile themselves to the lowered standard of living.

Fatalistic social structures

In extremely oppressive societies, people could lose the will to live and be prepared to die rather than continue in misery. Durkheim saw this form of suicide as 'of little contemporary importance', but one could see it in the actions of those in concentration camps during the Second World War.

Conclusions

Durkheim's work was taken to prove that suicide could only be understood in a social context, and not just as the decision of the individual. It was also given as a standard example of how to conduct sociological research.

The criticisms

The internal criticisms

There were various criticisms of Durkheim's methodology:

- His concept of social integration was too vague, he simply relied on intuitive ideas of what integration was.

- His variables of religion and the family were not as clear-cut as he suggested. How can these be 'isolated' as distinct influences on behaviour?

- The official statistics on which he based his research left something to be desired. For example, in Catholic countries where suicide is regarded as a sin, family doctors are reluctant to classify deaths as suicide.

However, the important point is that until the late 1960s no one seriously doubted Durkheim's general approach and conclusions.

The phenomenological criticisms

Durkheim has been strongly criticised by two writers, Douglas and Atkinson, who have accused him of assuming his 'interpretation' of suicide is correct, and ignoring the meaning the concept may have for others.

The meaning of suicide. Douglas points out that although one can define the *physical act* of a person taking his/her own life as suicide, this ignores the fact that suicide also has different *meanings* to those who take their own lives. Douglas suggests that those who commit suicide may define it in four possible ways (amongst others):

> *as a means of transforming the self*: this is where a person commits suicide as a means of gaining release from the cares of the world and entering paradise. An example of this was the mass suicide of followers of the religious leader Jim Jones in Guyana in 1978.
> *as a means of transforming oneself for others*: in this case suicide is a means of telling others how profound ones feelings are on a particular issue. For instance, a person who has caused a death through dangerous driving may commit suicide as a means of expressing his/her repentance.
> *as a means of achieving fellow feeling*: this is where the person is asking for help or sympathy and includes those sorts of 'suicides' where the person hopes to be found.
> *as a means of gaining revenge*: the person places the blame for his/her death on others. Usually, there is a note which accuses others of failing the person in some way.

The above shows that there is no single act which can be termed 'suicide'. It can only be defined as the physical state of self-administered death. But, the *meanings* which individuals place upon their acts are so different that is it

Bodies found at the Jonestown 'mass suicide'. The vat contains the deadly poison cyanide.

possible to place them all together in the one category? If there is no such one category of actions as suicide, but instead a whole range of meanings which are really very different, then the statistical comparisons of Durkheim become worthless. In some ways, this argument is very similar to the one put forward by Scheff in his discussion on the creation of mental illness (see p. 49).

The categorisation of suicides by coroners

Atkinson also develops the discussion on Durkheim's failure to understand that categories such as 'suicide' are really socially-constructed.

Before a death can be classified as suicide in Britain, a coroner must investigate the death at an inquest. The coroner's decision on whether the death was natural, accidental or suicide effectively determines, as far as the official statistics are concerned, what *really* is a suicide. Atkinson argues that the official statistics therefore reflect coroners' decisions and little else.

Obviously, only those who have killed themselves know exactly the motives and circumstances for their suicide.

In order to determine if a death was deliberate or not, the coroner must put together a series of 'clues' and then decide whether these suggest suicide. Atkinson suggests that the following are particularly important:

suicide notes: only 30 per cent of suicides leave notes, although it may be more and the family destroys them because of accusations (see above).

modes of death: some types of death are seen as clear indications of suicide, for example hanging, but others such as drowning present problems.

location and circumstances of death: coroners believe that suicides are committed in places and circumstances where they will not be discovered and where they are sure the outcome will be successful.

life history and mental condition: coroners believe that suicide is related to depression caused by some particular events (financial or emotional). Evidence to support this is therefore sought, together with information on the medical history.

If the evidence does not fit the commonsense model of the coroner, then suicide verdicts are not recorded. The verdict, therefore, reflects the assumptions of the coroner and his or her interpretations of the clues, rather than any 'reality'.

A brilliant young musician, Marcus Batchelor, was found hanged at his public school after an experiment that went tragically wrong. Marcus, aged 13, had been told by his trumpet teacher that he should imagine himself as a corpse in a coffin in order to understand a sombre piece of music.

The next day he was found hanging from a scarf tied to the ceiling and with his legs chained together.

Mr Roger Stokes, coroner, told an inquest at Yeovil, Somerset yesterday: "All the evidence suggests that he was trying to rehearse in his mind what it might feel like to be near death."

The coroner said Marcus was trying to gain an insight into a state of mind which would enable him to interpret music he was studying. He was absolutely sure that Marcus—"a happy, balanced young man"—did not take his own life. He recorded a verdict of accidental death.

Marcus, of Partridge Flat Road, Bessacarr, South Yorkshire, was in his second term as a music student at Wells Cathedral School, Somerset. He played trumpet, piano and cello.

The school's head of brass, Mr Ruari Wilson, said Marcus was an exceptionally talented pupil whose ambition was to be a professional composer and musician.

Source: 'Sombre "rehearsal" led to boy's death', article in *The Guardian*, 15 March, 1983

☐ 1 **How does the news item support the arguments of Atkinson and Douglas?**
2 **What alternative explanations could you offer if you were a different coroner 'reading between the lines'?**

☐ **PROJECT**

Prepare a 'content analysis' of your local newspapers over the last year—you can find microfiches or back copies in the main public libraries and in the offices of the newspapers. Take a sample of suicide reports, and then see if you can work out feasible alternative interpretations.

Ask if you could interview a reporter for a local newspaper who has written some suicide reports—what are his/her views?

What does the work of Atkinson and Douglas tell us about statistics in general?

Positivistic versus phenomenological approaches

The criticisms of Douglas and Atkinson illustrate a wider debate in sociology, between those who believe in using the methods of the natural sciences and who accept that there is a real, objective social world ready to be studied and measured (positivism), and those who believe that the social world is an insubstantial social creation which derives from the meanings that people create in their daily lives (phenomenological or subjective sociology).

☐ **ESSAYS**

1 **Durkheim viewed crime as both good and bad. Critically examine Durkheim's explanation of the two sides to crime.**

2 **The concept of *anomie* has been a major insight into the understanding of crime. What is anomie, and how has it changed in meaning over time? Illustrate your answer wherever possible with *contemporary* illustrations.**

3 **Sociology has traditionally been divided between those who stress that the only way to study society is through a 'positivistic' approach and those who seek a full understanding of 'meanings'— the subjective or phenomenological approach. The study of suicide is an excellent area to illustrate these debates. Explain how this can be so.**

Bibliography

R. Merton, *Social Structure and Anomie*, American Sociological Review, 1938 Vol. pp. 672–682

K. J. Erikson, *Wayward Puritans*, Wiley, 1966

J. D. Douglas, *The Social Meaning of Suicide*, Princeton University Press, 1967

J. M. Atkinson, *Societal Reactions to Suicide: the Role of Coroners' Definitions* in *Images of Deviance*, S. Cohen (ed), Penguin, 1971

3 · Subcultures, Places and Values

Subcultural and ecological approaches

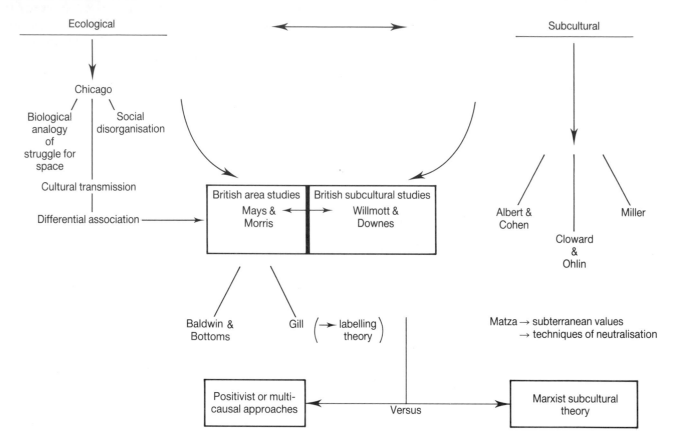

In this chapter a number of sociological explanations for criminal behaviour will be explored. These have had considerable importance in sociology. The actual explanations may appear to vary quite significantly, apparently having little in common. However, they are grouped together because they all stress the way that *groups of people create values* which both reflect their circumstances and influence their own behaviour. The sets of values or subcultures thus created are seen as the major influence in causing people to commit crime.

Firstly, we will undertake an examination of *ecological theories.* These stress the importance of studying particular areas of the cities to uncover the values generated in a particular neighbourhood which motivate people to commit crime.

Next, we move on to *subcultural theories*, which stress more the idea of distinctive values justifying crime, but which need not necessarily be generated in particular neighbourhoods. These are American in origin, so first we need to examine the theories and then see how they have been applied in Britain.

Finally, the later *positivist versions* of subcultural theory will be examined which derived from ecological and subcultural theories. These particular explanations have had considerable influence on policy-makers in Britain, and can be said to have paved the way for the contemporary Home Office approach to crime, based on *administrative sociology*, which is examined in detail in Chapter 11.

Ecological theories of crime

An enduring theme in sociological writing about crime has been the corrupting effect of city life. This view had developed particularly strongly in Europe during the nineteenth century, when cities were developing rapidly. Writers such as Durkheim and Tonïës had stressed the breakdown of the community, as this form of social interaction was altered under the twin pressures of urbanisation and industrialisation. People felt less 'bonded' to others and were more likely to look after their own selfish interests at the expense of others.

In the USA, urbanisation occurred later than in Europe and also took a different form in that cities developed as a result of massive waves of immigrants from Europe. Chicago had one of the biggest immigrant populations, rising from 10,000 in 1860 to 2,000,000 only fifty years later. It is not surprising, therefore, that the original urban studies were carried out by sociologists at the University of Chicago between 1914 and 1940. The work at Chicago University changed considerably over time, and one can distinguish a number of stages:

the biological analogy,
social disorganisation,
cultural transmission,
differential association.

The biological analogy

Initially, sociologists such as Park were strongly influenced by ideas of 'natural selection' and the 'struggle for space' concepts which were biologically-based and drawn from versions of the Darwinian theory of evolution. Park argued that cities were characterised by a 'biotic balance' in which communities developed, were disturbed (by new waves of immigration), and conflict occurred leading to a new form of community which replaced the original one. The struggle for space was linked to this. Individuals compete for the best habitats and those who lose out have to move (or remain) in the 'area of minimum choice', that is the city slums. However, allied to this biologically-based approach was the influence of 'symbolic interactionism', a sociological perspective which stressed the importance of examining social phenomena through the perspective of those involved. Rather than explaining behaviour totally from 'outside', the Chicago sociologists believed it was necessary to try to get into the minds of the people under study, to understand exactly why they were motivated to behave the way they did. Influenced by this they conducted detailed studies of life in the slums, endeavouring to portray how the individuals themselves saw life.

So, Chicago sociology was characterised by two quite distinct elements:
the *biological* approach, stressing 'natural' processes of struggle and domination,
the *sociological* approach, stressing the generation of meaning and culture by individuals through their interaction.

Social disorganisation

Park's work gave rise to the writing of Shaw and McKay who claimed

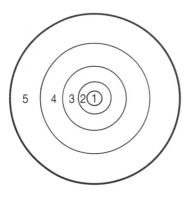

Zone 1 : 11.9%
Zone 2 : 8.8%
Zone 3 : 5.7%
Zone 4 : 3.3%
Zone 5 : 1.9%

The figures relate to South Chicago, USA. They show the proportion of delinquents as a percentage of the total male population in that zone aged between 10 and 16.

that Chicago (and other large cities) was divided into distinctive 'zones':

Zone 1: the central business district which had very few occupants but was the hub of commerce and banking during the day.

Zone 2: 'the interstitial zone' (or zone of transition). This was once an area of some considerable affluence, but had decayed and was characterised by multi-occupation use. This was the cheapest zone for housing and so new immigrants settled here first.

Zone 3: the respectable working class district. The district where the 'solid' working class lived.

Zone 4: suburbia—the pleasanter middle class districts further out of town.

Zone 5: the outer areas on the fringe of the city where the well-off live.

Shaw and McKay suggested that as each successive wave of immigrants arrived in the city, they were forced into the cheapest and least-desirable zone—that is, the zone of transition. As they settled and some were successful, they moved outward, with the less-successful remaining. Their places were taken by new waves of immigrants, and so the process started again.

When they examined the official crime rates for the city, Shaw and McKay noted that there were quite distinct patterns of crime, with Zone 2 being characterised by far higher rates than the rest of the city. This was not particularly surprising you might comment, but what was particularly interesting was that the *relative* crime rates remained similar over a long period of time, *even though the immigrant groups characterising Zone 2 had changed.* This means that it was not some natural criminal instincts on the part of, for example, Italians. It meant that each group living in the Zone—Poles, Irish, etc.—had similarly high rates of crime.

Shaw and McKay's explanation was that the high population turnover produced a state of 'social disorganisation', defined by two other writers of the Chicago School (Thomas and Znaniecki) as 'the decrease of the influence of existing social rules of behaviour upon individual members of the group'. This appears to mean that the informal mechanisms of social control that normally hold people back from deviant behaviour were weak or absent, and this 'released' people to commit criminal acts. These informal, restraining mechanisms include such things as public opinion, gossip and neighbourhood organisations.

The result of social disorganisation was that such things as prostitution, alcoholism, and crime flourished. This analysis has some definite echoes of Durkheim's ideas (see p. 16).

There was a degree of confusion however in Shaw and McKay's analysis in that crime and violence, for example, were seen both as *consequences* of social disorganisation and *evidence* of it. A little thought will show that this is a contradicition.

Cultural transmission

The next shift in the Chicago approach came in the later writings of Shaw and McKay, and was then taken up by Sutherland. Shaw and McKay radically altered the meaning of 'social disorganisation' to mean a distinctive (but coherent) set of values which provided alternative values to those of the mainstream society. This is quite distinct from earlier versions of social disorganisation which stressed the *lack* of coherent values. This new version of social disorganisation became known as the *cultural transmission* theory of delinquency, and clearly is the starting point for subcultural theory.

According to 'cultural transmission theory', in the most socially-disorganised and poorest zones of the city certain forms of crime have become the cultural norm transmitted from one generation to the next as part of the normal socialisation pattern. Successful criminals provided role models for the young, demonstrating both the possibilities of success through crime, and its normality.

Differential association

Although the theories of the 'Chicago School' had considerable influence, they were criticised at the time for being too vague. In an effort to 'tighten up' the explanation, Sutherland introduced his concept of *differential association*. This states that a person is likely to become criminal if he/she receives an 'excess of definitions favourable to violation of law over definitions unfavourable to violation of law'. Furthermore, definitions may vary in 'frequency, duration, priority and intensity'.

By this, Sutherland means that if people are surrounded by others who support law-breaking then they are likely to do so themselves. The variables in the model reflect the following:

> *frequency*: the number of times the definitions occur,
> *duration*: over what period of time,
> *priority*: eg, at what stage in life—the assumption is that childhood socialisation is more important than in later life,
> *intensity*: this refers to the prestige of the person making the definition.

Sutherland seems to be suggesting that some formula could be arrived at to work out exactly the combination of variables that would make a person commit a crime, yet this is clearly untestable. All the model shows is that those who commit crime have received the appropriate combination of variables and those who do not, have not! No predictions can be made.

British area studies

Chicago sociology has been immensely influential in a host of ways. One of these was to stimulate British 'area' studies. However, apart from the very early studies such as J. B. Mays' work in Liverpool, the theoretical orientation of the British studies moved steadily away from the concerns of the Chicago School.

Cultural transmission

In Mays' study of inner city Liverpool in the early 1950s, (*Growing Up in the City*), he found strong evidence to support many of Shaw and

McKay's findings. After interviewing boys (note, no females) from the Liverpool University Settlement Project, he concluded that the area possessed a particular culture in which shoplifting, theft and vandalism were accepted as normal by the local people. Mays also found the answer to a riddle that had puzzled sociologists for some time—why did only some of those people who were brought up in 'criminal neighbourhoods' turn to crime? Mays discovered that virtually *all* the local boys committed some kind of petty crime, but only *some* were caught.

Local authority housing policies

By the late 1950s when Morris conducted his study of Croydon (*The Criminal Area*), his findings pointed in a different direction. He did find that there were small 'pockets' of high delinquency rates, but there was no evidence that areas of high delinquency had any coherent set of values different from mainstream society. However, Morris suggested that a key factor in the concentration of delinquents in certain areas was related to the local council's policy of housing 'problem families' together in particular areas. These council estates also had the lowest rents, so that the poorest tended to choose them. The outcome was that those most likely to become delinquent anyway were placed together.

Housing classes

□ **Read the work of Rex and Moore to see how this idea was developed (see Bibliography for this chapter, p. 43).**

Other researchers were influenced by Morris' study and they rejected the idea of the Chicago sociologists that bad housing partially *caused* delinquency. Instead British studies focused their attention on the fact that there were *housing classes* in British cities who used their different levels of power and economic muscle to obtain the best housing stock in the most pleasant areas. Clearly, the least powerful and the poorest ended up with the worst housing. It was, therefore, predicatable that crime rates would be higher in the worst areas of the cities. The best example of this sort of research—though not directly in the field of criminology—was that of Rex and Moore in Sparkbrook, who showed how immigrants were trapped in the poorest inner city areas because they lost out in the competition between housing classes.

The theories tested

In one of the most detailed area studies in Britain, Baldwin and Bottoms studied the city of Sheffield. They divided the city into areas according to the most common form of housing—owner-occupier, council and privately-rented. The owner-occupier areas had significantly lower crime rates than the other two areas, even when social class differences were allowed for. Defining social disorganisation as areas with high levels of ethnic minorities, unmarried people, young adults and shared accommodation, they found that there was a relationship to (male) crime rates in privately-rented and owner-occupied, but not council areas. High population turnover was not associated with crime in any type of housing area.

Baldwin and Bottoms' work is ambiguous in its results, neither confirming previous studies in their entirety, nor rejecting them.

Interactionist

A further shift in the direction of area studies came in the work of Owen Gill, who brought an *interactionist* perspective to his study of inner city Liverpool. Gill describes the area called 'Luke Street', consisting of an unattractive council estate which was used for problem families by the local council. It soon gained a reputation for toughness and trouble, so that 'respectable' families would avoid living there if possible. The reputation of the street had other consequences too for its inhabitants. For example, employers would be reluctant to give jobs to people who lived there and credit was difficult to obtain. The residents self-perceptions were influenced by their reputation, and Gill suggests that local residents may have felt the necessity to live up to their tough reputation. The police too had a negative view of the area, and Gill claims that they were 'sensitised' to potential trouble there, so that their actions often led to greater lawlessness than would have been the case, had they treated Luke Street like any other area. The activities of the police were, therefore, *amplifying deviance*.

☐ **PROJECT**

It is clearly impossible to conduct a full 'area study' of your town/city. But you could:

a) use a map of your town to see if there are distinctive zones;
b) interview local housing officials about: (i) policy in your town; (ii) are there 'problem' areas? If so why?
c) interview the police. Do they see certain parts of the town as greater problems than others?

Subcultural Theories

Chicago sociology directed attention towards the *motivations* which delinquents had. It put forward the novel idea, still rejected by many, that there is nothing 'wrong' with delinquents, rather they perceive the world in a different way and act accordingly. Delinquents then have a distinct set of values which guide their behaviour in the same way that you and I are guided by our more conventional ideas. The existence of a distinctive set of values within the main culture of society is known as a *subculture*.

Status frustration

The first explicit use of the concept of subculture is found in the work of Albert Cohen, writing in the mid–1950s (*Delinquent Boys, The Culture of the Gang*). Cohen was puzzled by the fact that most delinquent acts were not motivated by economic ends. Vandalism or graffiti spraying, for example, brings no economic benefit to the perpetrator. His answer was that most delinquents are motivated by *status deprivation*, wherein they feel they are looked down upon by the rest of society and denied any status. They therefore develop a distinct set of values or a subculture which provides them with alternative ways of gaining status, and possibly leads them into delinquency.

☐ **PROJECT**

A way of researching Cohen's argument would be to question lower and higher stream school students concerning their attitudes to school and their feelings about teachers and other pupils. A useful starting point for research would be to read parts of David Hargreaves' *Social Relations in the Secondary School*, RKP, 1967, or Stephen Ball's *Beachside Comprehensive*, CUP, 1981, where just this form of research is undertaken. (See Bibliography p. 43.)

Those who are most likely to commit deviant acts are generally found in the lower streams of schools, living in deprived areas and having the worst chances in the job market. It is the effect of school, however, that is most profound in its influence on the delinquents. Cohen argues that for adolescents the primary agency awarding (and denying) status is school. Those in the top streams are rewarded and feel important, while those in the lowest streams are aware that they are looked upon as the most stupid, the least interesting and with little to offer teachers or society. Aware that they are branded failures by society in general, Cohen argues that the lower stream boys (note girls are not even discussed by Cohen!) therefore develop their own subculture with its own values. The subculture is based on a deliberate reversal of accepted forms of behaviour, so those actions such as stealing, rudeness, violence etc which are condemned in the wider society are elevated to a central position in the boys' subculture. The subculture, it should be noted, is a *collective* response to status denial.

The subculture has two uses for the lower stream boys. First, it creates an alternative set of values against which boys can measure their behaviour, so that they can compete within this for status amongst their peers. Second, it provides a means of striking back at society—in Cohen's words 'there is a kind of malice apparent, an enjoyment of the discomfiture of others'. Petty theft and vandalism, for example, provide delinquents with a measure of revenge.

Cohen is, therefore, arguing that delinquents are no different from other adolescents in seeking status and they are simply resolving the need to gain status through their delinquent acts.

Illegitimate opportunity structure

An attempt to link Merton's anomie (see p. 16) and subcultural theory was made by Cloward and Ohlin. Merton had suggested that individuals turned to crime, drug addiction and violence when society provided too few opportunities to attain legally the socially-approved goals set by society.

However, Cloward and Ohlin felt that Merton had ignored the existence of an *illegitimate opportunity structure* that ran parallel to the legal one. This had three levels:

> *criminal subculture,*
> *conflict subculture,*
> *retreatist subculture.*

The *criminal opportunity structure* exists when the following conditions hold. First, there is a stable, cohesive working-class community with contacts in both the mainstream legal community and the illegal one. This enables stolen goods to be sold through the wider community, for example. Second, there has to be successful role models, people from the local community who have done well from crime, achieving a high standard of living from their illegal activities. This provides an example of success through crime. Third, there needs to be a career structure for aspiring criminals. This involves movement by age group through the various career grades. For example, starting at about ten by stealing car aerials, then on to stealing radios at

fourteen, the entire car at seventeen and possibly then entering organised crime in their early twenties.

This form of subculture provides working class males with an alternative to the legitimate job market.

In the *conflict subculture* however, if the conditions just mentioned are absent and there is no career in crime available to young males, they may turn their frustration at certain failure in both the legitimate and illegitimate opportunity structures into violence. This is the cause of the sort of gang warfare which appears to be a hallmark of the slums of New York.

The *retreatist subculture* is the final level of the illegal opportunity structure and is the one that takes the double failures, who could not make it in crime or violence. These failures 'retreat' into drugs and alcoholism, paid for by petty theft, shoplifting and prostitution.

Criticisms

This approach has been criticised for making the same assumption as Merton, that everyone seeks the same goal of financial success. Instead, it is argued there are a wide variety of goals that people aim at, so that failure cannot simply be explained in terms of lack of financial success. A second major problem for this argument is that there is no evidence to support the idea of subcultures as described by Cloward and Ohlin. As we shall see later (p. 39), coherent subcultures like these do not appear to exist in Britain.

Delinquency as the consequence of normal working class values

Both Cohen's theories and those of Cloward and Ohlin, suggest that crime is the result of distinctive subcultures which provide alternative guidelines to action from the mainstream culture. A different approach was supplied by Miller (*Lower Class Culture as a Generating Milieu of Gang Delinquency*). Miller suggests that there are six focal concerns of working class culture which can lead working class males into crime. His point, therefore, is that crime is an extension of *normal working class values*, not a distinctive set of *alternative* values.

The six focal concerns are:

trouble: they accept that life involves violence and they will not run away from fights,

toughness: males ought to demonstrate the qualities of 'manliness', being able to drink, womanise, play sport etc,

smartness: this involves 'looking good' and being 'sharp',

excitement: they are always on the look out for some 'fun' and enjoyment,

fate: they believe that there is little that can be done about their lives, whatever will be, will be.

autonomy: although they can do little about the general conditions of their lives, they do not want anybody to 'push them around', so they resent authority when presented in the form of the police or a boss.

☐ **Do these focal concerns exist? If they do who holds them (class, ethnic, gender, age differences?) Devise a set of questions which will provide 'indicators' to measure them. Is there any way of comparing behaviour against the answers you obtain? Is this important?**

Howard Parker's study of a group of Liverpool adolescents (*View from the Boys*) helps to illustrate these ideas. The 'boys' (as they call themselves) go out for a night out. They aren't looking for trouble (fights), but should anyone hint that they aren't tough or they can't take their drinks 'like men', then a fight ensues. On these nights out, the boys ability to pick up girls often depends on how they look, and their wit and repartee (smartness). The essence of a good night out is to have 'a laff' (excitement), but when they go out they have no idea what's going to happen (fate), but they don't want to be pushed around by 'bouncers' or policemen (autonomy).

One of the problems with this analysis of crime is that it stresses these are *working class values*, but a moment's reflection shows that these values are distributed *throughout society* and are as likely to be found amongst the middle class members of a rugby team, as amongst the working class 'boys'.

Delinquency and ordinary behaviour

Most subcultural approaches to deviance had two clear characteristics: they emphasised the idea of subcultures as distinct sets of values from those held by the majority of the population; and that delinquents were propelled into their actions by subcultural forces stronger than themselves, known as *determinism.* Yet, research in Britain has rarely found any of the elusive ingredients of the distinctive subculture— indeed they have merely shown how *ordinary* delinquents are.

Matza in *Delinquency and Drift* rejected both these underlying assumptions. He claimed that delinquents were similar to everyone else in their values and voiced similar feelings of outrage about crime in general as the majority of society. When caught, he pointed out, they express feelings of remorse and extend justifications for their acts.

Subterranean values

The first point Matza makes is that we all hold two levels of values. The values that guide us most of the time are the respectable, conventional ones, in which we play the good roles of father, daughter, teacher etc, but there are occasions when the underlying (subterranean) values of sexuality, greed and aggressiveness emerge. The most obvious example is the Christmas party, when the hidden lusts in the office (or college) emerge for one drunken afternoon—life then returns to normal on the return to work the following week! These subterranean values then are generally controlled, but *all of us hold them* and *occasionally* all of us *give vent to them.* Matza suggests that delinquents are simply more likely to behave according to subterranean values in 'inappropriate' situations.

☐ **Matza is rather vague about the actual content of the subterranean values. Can you suggest what subterranean values may consist of?**

Techniques of neutralisation

If delinquents are as much committed to conventional values as anyone else and furthermore express condemnation of similar crimes to their own (but committed by others), why on earth should they commit them at all? In answer, Matza suggests that delinquents are able to put forward justifications for their particular crimes as exceptions to the general rule. 'Yes, what I did is wrong, but ...' Matza argues that there are five justifications or *techniques of neutralisation*:

Denial of responsibility: It is not the culprit's fault, something made him/her do it, for example, 'I was drunk.'
Denial of victim: The crime in general is wrong, but the victim in this particular case deserved it, for example 'bloody Pakis, I hate them'.
Denial of injury: The victim is seen as not being harmed in any way by the crime, for example 'they can afford it'.
Condemnation of condemners: This is where the delinquent argues that the accusers are no different than he/she, for example, 'Yeah, I was driving when drunk, but so does everybody else—even you'.
Appeal to higher loyalties: The delinquent claims that he/she had to do it because of some general 'moral' standard, for example, 'I couldn't leave my mates (during a fight)'.

Techniques of neutralisation then, act as a *justification* why the general rules can be broken.

Drift

The final element in his explanation for delinquency is that of *drift*. If we all hold subterranean values, and we could all justify our actions if necessary, why is it that only some young people commit crime? Matza suggests that youth is a period in 'no mans land', not yet adult but no longer a child. Youths feel that they lack any control over their own lives, and they long to gain some power over their destiny. According to Matza, this period of drift loosens the adolescent from the constraining bonds of society (note that the bonds are *loosened*, no more), so he/she is more susceptible to suggestions of deviant acts by the peer group. Finally, in an effort to show that he/she has control over his/her life, the youth may commit a delinquent act. However, there is

□ **Is it possible to 'operationalise' Matza's concept of 'drift'? If so, how would you do it? If you think it's not possible, explain your reasons and then discuss whether the theory is of any use if it is untestable.**

no deviant career, the youth is not committed in any way to a life of crime, and he/she tends to drift out of crime again, for instance when they have a decent job.

This last concept of drift is unsatisfactory in at least one respect. If the youth wishes to gain control over his/her destiny, why commit a delinquent act? Won't any act do?

A second problem with Matza's theory is that there is no attempt to place delinquency within any wider framework (or *structural location*) of economic and social circumstances that drive male working-class youth into greater levels of delinquency than anyone else.

British subcultural studies

Attempts to uncover British subcultures were made in Britain too, although the perspective always remained entangled with the concept of 'area studies'. Indeed many of the 'area studies' mentioned earlier could equally well be placed under the heading of subculture, particularly the earlier work of J. B. Mays, who pointed the finger at the power of the family and peer group in socialising young people in deviant attitudes.

Looking for fun?

However, few studies supported Mays' conviction that distinctive subcultures existed predisposing certain working class children to commit crime. Willmott studied adolescent males in a working class district of London (*Adolescent boys in East London*) and could find little evidence to substantitiate the existence of a delinquent subculture.

Willmott suggested instead that there were two elements to explain the delinquency of working class youths. First, the youths in his study had generally boring lives, with uninteresting, dead-end jobs. In order to compensate for this, they would be on the look out for some fun and excitement. This sometimes led them into law breaking activities—but they were rarely planned, nor were they motivated by economic reward.

A second aspect of their lives was that they were far more *visible* than middle class youth. The small homes and lack of private space meant that 'hanging around' on street corners or in cafes was the only possibility if they wanted to meet together. This brought their 'horseplay' to the attention of passers-by, and more importantly, the police. Minor infractions of the law were, therefore, more likely to be punished, simply because they were under the observation of the police.

Dissociation

Downes, too, conducted a thorough study of East London adolescents, and tested the American subcultural theories. There was no evidence to support the existence of status frustration, or of the 'illegitimate opportunity structure' of Cloward and Ohlin. Downes did find strong evidence to support the insights of Matza, however.

The lives of working class adolescents were characterised by *dissociation* from work and aspirations for a career. For them, employment was merely a means of obtaining money, they neither hoped for nor received satisfaction from their employment. However, Downes points out that the adolescents showed no resentment about their low school status (see Cohen), nor their lack of employment opportunities (see Cloward and Ohlin). The lack of satisfaction at work and school led the youths to stress what Downes terms 'leisure values', which bear considerable resemblance to Matza's 'subterranean values'. These are the underlying values of 'having a good time' which are present throughout British culture. The youths in the study place much greater stress on leisure values than middle class youths precisely because of their relative lack of satisfaction at school and at work. The result is that they are more disposed to commit petty acts of crime in the process of enjoying themselves. There is, though, no commitment to deviant values.

The end of conventional subcultural theory

Downes' study really marked the deathknell of the conventional subcultural/ecological approach, although there were two studies after this by Patrick and Parker. However, these moved a significant distance from the traditional approach and could be taken to indicate the splitting of the subculture into positivistic and Marxist strands.

In his exciting study of street gangs in Glasgow, (*A Glasgow Gang Observed*), Patrick concluded that there were fairly tightly-organised gangs there, which he argued were formed around a particularly strong psychotic individual who led the gang and maintained discipline. This is so different from most other subcultural studies, that we will have to conclude that this form of gang is peculiar to Glasgow, as there is no evidence to support this in other sociological work.

The second study was Howard Parker's excellent *View from the Boys*. Parker studied a group of delinquent youths in inner city Liverpool who made their living from stealing 'catseyes' (car radios). He found little evidence to support any of the conventional theories and instead suggested that a *structural* Marxist analysis was needed to understand the situation and the views of the 'boys' in his study.

These two studies also illustrate the splintering of subcultural theory into two theoretically opposed camps of *positivist* and *Marxist* subculture.

Positivist ('empirical' or 'multi-causal') approach

This stressed the search for the *differences* in background and upbringing between delinquents and 'normal' youth. We will examine this in the next section.

Marxist subculture

This stressed that the subcultures develop in response to the structural inequalities in society. Working class youths face specific problems and they try to resolve these by creating youth subcultures, some of which can lead to crime. These are examined on pages 79–90.

Positivist approaches

Positivism is the theoretical *method* which copies, in a modified form, the methodology of the natural sciences.

In criminology, the method involves comparing the deviant with the normal person and searching for the differences between them. These differences are then assumed to have *caused* the delinquency.

It could be argued that much of the subcultural theory we have looked at so far follows this methodology implicitly. However, one strand of British sociology from the late 1950s onward *explicitly* followed this path. The studies found that no one variable could be isolated to explain crime, but that there were a host of shifting variables which seemed to be different with each youth or group of youths. The sociologists with this perspective argued that there were no specific factors causing an individual to commit crime, instead it was a *varying mixture* of different factors that was responsible. The term *multi-causal* approach was therefore adopted.

The approach derives from the later work of J. B. Mays.

> *It may be that they were brought up without proper control and supervision, that they were allowed to mix with street corner groups and conformed to the partially delinquent norms of their associates. It may be that they found themselves depressed by continued experiences of failure at school and elsewhere and developed chip-on-shoulder attitudes which made them resentful of authority and ... ready to indulge in hooliganism against the respectable law-abiding society ... It could also arise from a combination of these processes. (J. B. Mays,* Juvenile Delinquency, the Family and the Social Group, Longman, 1972.*)*

Probably the best-known work has been by West and Farrington (*The Delinquent Way of Life*). They belong to the Cambridge School of

Criminology. In a large-scale study of 411 working class boys from the age of eight to the age of nineteen, they isolated the following five factors as being particularly associated with delinquency:

low family income,
large-size family,
comparatively low intelligence,
having a parent with a criminal record,
having parents considered to be unsatisfactory in rearing children.

As the boys moved through their teens, the authors also noted that males with the backgrounds shown above were more likely to show evidence of 'aggression, unstable work records, anti-establishment attitudes, driving after heavy drinking, heavy gambling, drug use, involvement in anti-social groups, sexual activity, immoderate smoking, hanging about, and being tattooed'. No attempt is made by the authors to *explain* the origin of these values apart from noting that they are linked to the five factors above. This approach is merely meant to produce a set of factors to predict which sort of children are likely to become delinquent.

Later models of multi-causal explanations for crime have gone beyond West and Farrington by incorporating psychological and even biological elements. In the United States, for example, Patterson has done intensive work on the psychology of the family, to show how parent–child interaction can help to produce delinquent children. In an enormous study of delinquency in Britain, Rutter and Giller throw together every psychological, ecological and sociological theory known and conclude that they all have something to say. Quite where this takes us it is difficult to know!

Sexism: Invisible females

In this chapter there are no references to females, which reflects the *invisibility* of girls in sociological research at this time. Females were excluded from the study for a number of reasons. These include:

the fact that the majority of sociologists were male, which meant that: a) they were interested in *male* areas of interest, which delinquency was seen to be and; b) they found it easier to study the male world of all-male gangs;
official statistics indicated that crime was a male activity—though it is interesting that there was no serious sociological study to find out why.

In chapter 7 we will examine theories of female criminality in some detail.

Youth cultural studies are only one example of what has been called the 'male norm' in social science research. The predominant focus on young men has rendered young women either totally invisible, or, at best, marginal to theoretical analysis. Young men's experiences have been presented as the norm against which young women must be judged. This has had two unfortunate consequences: most youth studies have developed gender (i.e. male) specific theories which have been presented as universally relevant to all young people; and many researchers have struggled with considerable difficulty to 'fit' young women's experiences into appropriate and unsatisfactory models which have been developed from a male perspective.

One study followed 25 young white working-class women from Birmingham fifth forms into their first two years in the local job market.

They were visited every two or three months at home, in local coffee bars and pubs, and their workplaces wherever possible. The researchers talked to their mothers, sisters and girlfriends but male relatives and friends were far more elusive. Ten case studies were done of young women's workplaces, covering traditionally 'female work' in offices and factories, and 'men's jobs' in engineering. As youth unemployment levels began to rise sharply, the study included interviews with those young women who had experienced prolonged periods of unemployment.

However, there were problems with trying to use the 'gang of lads' model.

Most young men 'hung around' in those 'gangs of lads' which have provided the foundation for so many studies of youth cultures and subcultures. Young women either had one extremely close 'best' girlfriend, or spent their time with a small group of two, three or four female friends. Some of these friendships had lasted for years, especially between 'best' girlfriends, but the membership of female friendship groups could change suddenly if young women shifted their allegiances elsewhere.

The different social structure of most female friendship groups made it extremely difficult to pinpoint specific 'gangs' or large groups with clearly identifiable styles and shared cultural values. Female friendships were both more fluid and more intense than young men's, and there were few obvious female equivalents to the 'gang of lads' model.

The definition of conformity and deviance in school was very different for young women compared to their male peers. 'Deviance' for young men tends to centre around their perceived levels of verbal and physical aggression: being identified as a 'troublemaker' can also have positive connotations for a young man's masculinity, admitting him to a group of 'hard' lads. 'Deviance' for young women is usually defined in relation to their sexuality, so that to be labelled as a 'troublemaker' can be associated with being too feminine and too (hetero)sexual—a slag. Thus the implications of cultural resistance in school are quite different for young working-class women and men.

Source: Adapted from *It's Different for Girls*, Social Studies Review, November 1986

☐ 1 **Why have there been so few 'female' youth studies?**
2 **Are the 'male models' of troublemakers useful for understanding females? Explain your answer.**
3 **Examine the methodology used—how else could you research female youth culture? Why did she use her chosen methods, do you think?**

It has been suggested that the characteristics often attributed to delinquents are largely due to the processes of criminal justice. All youngsters break laws on occasion, and if they come from a deprived background, continual law breaking may be a sensible solution to this. The implication here is that delinquency is a normal response and delinquents are no different from their social equals. If they appear different this is because the system tends to pick out odd individuals—such as children from broken homes—for official action. Once officially labelled as delinquents, the disapproval they get from teachers, employers, parents and girl friends insures that these scapegoats of the system live up to the bad name they have been given.

In order to prove that delinquents really are different from their fellows, two things must be studied from an early age to show that the characteristics of the delinquent minority are present before they appear in the courts, and so cannot be due to the baleful effects of police and court labelling ...

The study was based on 411 boys. They represented an unselected sample of local schoolboys living in a traditional working class area of London. They were intensively studied from eight to ten years old, and have been monitored up to the age of nineteen. The early information about the boys and their backgrounds has been used to find out the distinguishing characteristics of those who later became juvenile delinquents. A boy was counted an official delinquent if he acquired an entry in the Criminal Record Office.

In effect one-fifth of the boys became juvenile delinquents .... The delinquents were always the less-favoured group. For example, those more likely to become delinquents were the unpopular boys rather than the popular ones: those with high 'neuroticism' scores, rather than low; those from broken homes rather than those from intact homes; those with nervous mothers rather than those with healthy mothers; and those born illegitimate rather than those born to married parents. This confirmed that delinquents do, in fact, differ from, and are in many ways inferior to or less fortunate than, their non-delinquent schoolfellows.

... we judged five factors to have special importance: low family income, large family, comparatively low intelligence, having a parent with a criminal record, and having parents considered to be unsatisfactory in rearing children ... the chances of a boy having more than one conviction as a juvenile were more than six times greater if three or more of those adverse factors were present ...

In order to produce a measure of delinquent behaviour independent of official records, the boys were given a questionnaire about their own behaviour ... As far as could be judged boys tended to respond surprisingly frankly and truthfully to this test ... the overlap between the boys identified as delinquent by self-report and the official delinquents was very great: forty-one out of the eighty self-reported delinquents were among the eighty-four official delinquents. The thirty-nine boys with high self-report scores, but no juvenile convictions were separately examined. A disproportionately large number of these had had contacts with the police as juveniles or had got an official conviction record as young adults, or had got an official conviction record as young adults ...

However, they did not share to any great extent many of the characteristics of official delinquents. For instance, they did not come from low income families or tend to have low intelligence. In their cases it seemed probable that official prosecutions were avoided or delayed because of their background characteristics.

Source: West, '*Are Delinquents Different*', Heinemann, 1977

☐ 1 **What type(s) of theoretical approach to the study of crime underlies this extract? Please give evidence to support your answer.**

2 **What approach is being argued against here?**

3 **What sort of methodology was used in the survey?**

4 **What is a self-report test? In what circumstances are they generally used?**

5 **Briefly summarise West's key arguments.**

6 **On reading this extract, it seemed to me there was a contradiction, or at least a weakness in the central arguments of the text, that emerges from the evidence of the last paragraph. Does there seem any problem to you? If so, please explain it.**

☐ **ESSAYS**

1 **Ecological theories have had a long and complicated theoretical journey from Chicago to Britain. Explain what ecological theories are, and examine how they have changed. Illustrate your answer with reference to relevant studies.**

2 **Critically examine subculture as a useful explanation of delinquency.**

3 **Take two studies of delinquency, one from a traditional subcultural stance, the other from a positivistic perspective. Critically compare them.**

Bibliography

R. E. Park, *Human Ecology*, American Journal of Sociology, July, 1936

C. R. Shaw and H. D. McKay, *Juvenile Delinquency and Urban Areas*, University of Chicago Press, 1942

E. H. Sutherland and D. R. Cressey, *Principles of Criminology*, Lippincott, 1974

J. B. Mays, *Growing up in the City*, Liverpool University Press, 1954

J. B. Mays, *Crime and the Social Structure*, Faber, 1967

J. Rex and R. Moore, *Race, Community and Conflict*, Oxford University Press, 1967

J. Richardson and J. Lambert, *The Sociology of Race*, Causeway Press, 1985

J. Baldwin and A. E. Bottoms, *The Urban Criminal: A Study in Sheffield*, Tavistock, 1976

O. Gill, *Luke Street*, Macmillan, 1977

A. Cohen, *Delinquent Boys, the Culture of the Gang*, The Free Press, 1955

D. Willmott, *Adolescent Boys in East London*, RKP, 1966

J. Patrick, *A Glasgow Gang Observed*, Eyre-Methuen, 1973

Labelling theory derives from the 'symbolic interactionist' school of sociology. This originated towards the end of the last century in the writings of Cooley and, later, Mead. In essence, symbolic interactionism was a revolt against the positivist approach which viewed society as objective and 'real'. In the positivist model, people were seen to be totally controlled by society and had little autonomy. They were like puppets with 'society' pulling the strings.

Symbolic interactionism stressed the way that people actively go about creating their own worlds, making choices and altering their behaviour according to their own perceptions of the situation. Far from being some all-powerful controlling force, society was seen as the product of people's *interactions*.

The use of the word *symbol* in the term 'symbolic interactionism' points to the way that the world consists of *symbols* to which we attach meaning and then respond. A simple example of a symbol is a red traffic light. This 'tells' us to stop if we are driving a car. The point is, of course, there is nothing intrinsic in a red light that says we *have* to stop. It is merely a symbol which we understand and respond to. Furthermore, the symbol can be ignored in certain situations—an ambulance racing to the scene of an accident, for example.

A red traffic light is an inanimate symbol, but we respond to symbols attached to people as well. So we have expectations and particular ways of behaving towards a doctor, a mother, a next door neighbour, etc even though this may be the same person in different roles.

Symbolic interactionists argue that we are brought up to recognise symbols attached to things and people and to respond in what we regard as appropriate ways. The responses are not fixed, or determined by society, but are open to negotiation by us. Society consists of people responding to, and negotiating over, symbols.

This may well be interesting you say, but what are the implications for crime? Well, more positivistic approaches start from the viewpoint that only a small proportion of the population commit deviant and criminal acts. If we make the assumption that people act the way they do because they are 'propelled' by social forces beyond their control, then presumably if we can isolate those social forces, we can find the 'causes' of their anti-social behaviour. The result of this approach is to blame parental upbringing or a delinquent peer group, or the nature of the capitalist economy etc.

The alternative approach which developed from symbolic interactionism has been called *labelling theory.* This is generally associated with the work of Howard Becker and to a lesser extent, Edwin Lemert.

Becker argues that the central questions for the study of deviance and rule-breaking are:

a) how individuals become labelled as deviant and the consequences for that person of being so labelled: *the processes of labelling and the deviant career;*
b) how certain acts come to be defined as deviant and the consequences of this: *the process of law creation.*

To make our discussion of labelling as clear as possible, I intend to explain these two areas and then to use the examples of:

mental illness,
the role of the mass media in deviancy amplifiation,
the creation of the concept of juvenile delinquency, and
the passing of the law to make smoking marihuana illegal

to illustrate: a) the importance of labelling in the study of deviance and; b) to highlight how different its insights are from other approaches.

The labelling of individuals

Writers such as Becker and Lemert have pointed out the important fact that most of us commit deviant acts at one time or another and yet we continue to regard those who are caught as somehow different from the rest of us. Yet, for labelling theorists the only difference between the bulk of the population and criminals is that criminals get caught!

A story from Box's book *Deviance, Reality and Society* will illustrate this. Box once found himself selected for jury duty. The trial was fairly mundane and consisted of a theft charge concerning a very small amount of money. After a short deliberation the jury agreed that the defendent was guilty. Having finished their duty as citizens the members of the jury then relaxed, and in a matter-of-fact way began to discuss how they would fiddle their travelling and out of pocket expenses, by claiming inflated amounts. Box points out that most people on the jury actually 'fiddled' more money than the woman they had just convicted of theft had stolen!

The difference then between being a criminal and being an upright citizen is the fact that a person is labelled as such. The application of a label to someone has significant consequences for how that person is treated by others and perceives him/herself.

Effects of labelling: how a person is treated by others

We live in a world in which we categorise people and then respond to them according to the label. Teachers label pupils as good or troublemaker and then act accordingly by rewarding and punishing, the casual acquaintance is labelled as interesting or boring and we seek out their company or avoid them based on this.

A good example of the power of labelling comes from Lemert's distinction between primary and secondary deviance. In his study of stuttering, Lemert found that stuttering was common in only one 'tribe' of North American Pacific Coast Indians, and it was unknown in all the others. Lemert observed that public oratory was extremely important in the tribe with high levels of stuttering, indeed to attain the status of 'manhood', oratory was necessary. If young boys showed any speech defect the parents reacted with such concern and horror that the child became sensitised to his defect and worried about it. His nervousness would be so great, argued Lemert that it would *cause* him to stutter.

We can see here that the primary deviance of a speech defect was not particularly important, but the effect of the worried parents *labelling* the child a stutterer was important, and caused the nervousness that actually led to the stuttering (the secondary deviance).

So people are labelled in various ways by others and then reacted to accordingly. This has consequences which labelling theorists suggest are more important than the original deviance.

Variability. The process of labelling someone is not straightforward or based on some clear-cut laws, after all the person who interests you may bore me and vice-versa, while the unemployed youth who steals from a large chain store may evoke sympathy in one person and anger in another. Labelling can be said to be variable, with the application of a label to someone varying with such diverse factors as place, gender, age and so on.

An example of this is Kitsuse's study of responses to homosexuals. In his research, he asked mature students about their responses to homosexuals whom they had met, or who had made advances to them. The definitions of what constituted 'typical' homosexual behaviour, or what actions had signified homosexual advances, varied astonishingly. One student claimed that when he was in the army he knew an officer was homosexual because he had been pleasant to ordinary troops. Another student claimed that a man he had met in a bar was obviously homosexual because he had wanted to talk about psychology! Yet other students had defined acquaintances kissing them as merely signs of friendship. Responses too varied considerably, from violent rejections of presumed advances to no change in attitude whatsoever.

The point here is that what is seen to constitute deviance varies widely and there are no agreed levels at which labels are attached.

Negotiable. Furthermore, we often change our mind about people and then decide as a result to re-label them. After half an hour with the 'bore' we realise that he or she is actually quite interesting, merely shy. It is not true either that a person has no control over the label placed upon them by others. Labelling theorists point out that some people may have the power to reject a negative label, while others are unable

☐ **There are a number of ways of finding out how people respond differently to awkward, embarrassing or deviant situations. You could devise a simple questionnaire consisting of two stages. First, what they define as deviant or odd. Second, how they would respond to hypothetical 'deviant' situations which you present them with. A more radical (and more difficult) activity is to set up an experiment. Create a deviant situation (a loud argument in public, or a pretend fight?). Observe the various responses of the 'audience'. Interview them afterwards to see how they interpreted the situation.**

to muster enough resources to deny the negative label and so must accept it.

An example of how labels can be rejected comes from Reiss' work on boy homosexual prostitutes. The boys developed a strict code of honour in which they were not allowed to enjoy their activities and anyone who did was immediately thrown out of the group. The boys perceived themselves, and were perceived by others in the group as heterosexual, finding little difficulty rejecting the label of homosexual through their aggressiveness and the code of honour.

Master status. Becker uses this term to describe how once a label is applied to someone (child-molester or violent criminal), all the actions that a person performs or has performed in the past are interpreted in the light of the label.

Effects of labelling: how people perceive themselves

Cooley, writing near the end of the last century, had suggested that a good way to describe how we see ourselves is *the looking glass self.* By this he meant that we build our identity primarily as a result of how others act and respond towards us. If people comment on how ugly I am, or what a large nose I have and how spotty my skin is, then I am likely to see a big-nosed, spotty, rather ugly man in the mirror and to think of myself that way. This view of my *self* will influence how I act towards other people. For example, I will probably lack confidence in my dealings with the opposite sex and may revert to writing books as a result!

Career. Becker suggested that the process by which people take on an identity given to them by others, could be regarded as a 'career'. We normally use the term career when we are talking about employment, and it means a gradual climb up the ladder to finally reach the point where one can say 'I made it'. At this stage the person may have achieved his/her aim in life, for example, of being a successful solicitor.

Becker suggests that this process is going on all the time in the area of deviance too, as people gradually attain the status of being anything from a drug addict to a child abuser.

Labelling theory

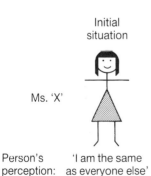

Ms. 'X'

Initial situation

Person's perception: 'I am the same as everyone else'

Label applied to individual: people act differently

'*Why* are they treating me like this?'

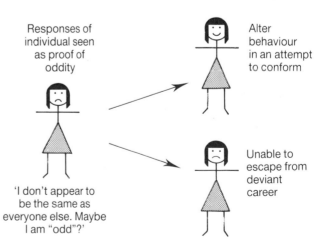

Responses of individual seen as proof of oddity

'I don't appear to be the same as everyone else. Maybe I am "odd"?'

Alter behaviour in an attempt to conform

Unable to escape from deviant career

1. Why did Ms. 'X' get labelled in the first place? Surely she must be odd to be picked out?

2. Why do some people escape the deviant career and others remain trapped in it?

Clearly the career cannot progress without other people labelling a person and then responding to them in such a way that eventually they learn that that is their identity (or master status). They then begin to act in a manner which reflects this perception of themselves. In turn this final acceptance of the label and adjustment of behaviour will confirm to others that they were right all along.

You will see this process of career being examined in the study of mental illness on page 51–53.

All these ideas are pulled together in the diagram on page 47.

Many police officers come from the lower middle or upper working class. The values upon which the culture of the lower ranks is based seem to have evolved from the notions of respectability which are important in this section of society. "It is a milieu in which people who do not speak with a London or other regional accent, and men who do not dress like football managers, are definitely made to feel out of place." Coming from the respectable stratum, many police officers, say the PSI, are preoccupied with reinforcing the distinction between their kind of decent, rate-paying, property-owning, law-abiding citizens and the "slag". It is important that police officers should not interpret such a description of common police attitudes as sarcastic or condescending. Every group has its distinctive values and these ones are shared by most of the population. "Slag", for the London police, includes people who are dependent on drugs, live in communes or squats, hold unusual political opinions or have unusual sexual habits. Certain council housing estates are thought to accommodate a lot of "slag". As the researchers show, when dealing with people who are respectable, or anyone who evokes their sympathy, ordinary police officers can deploy social skills of great sensitivity and wisdom ...

One reason for the disparagement of black people is that English criteria of respectability have not yet adjusted so as to differentiate between more and less respectable black people and to incorporate the former within local neighbourhood communities. Another is the self-fulfilling element in police beliefs about black criminality. The latest national survey by PSI found that the unemployment rate among young men of West Indian origin is around 50 per cent. Racial discrimination, especially in recruitment to employment, continues at a high level. Perhaps in part because of these circumstances young black people more frequently commit crimes of theft from the person than members of other ethnic groups. Probably more of them use cannabis. So police officers infer that, other things being equal, if they stop a young black man in the street they are more likely to find evidence of a crime than if they stop a young white man. Colour becomes a self-fulfilling criterion.

There is a vicious circle of reasoning from inadequate evidence which cannot easily be rectified either by training or supervision. It has a further unfortunate twist in that this preconception operates to the particular disadvantage of black men seen in the more respectable neighbourhoods. Thus one constable observed: "If I saw a black man walking through Wimbledon High Street I would definitely stop him. 'Course, down here it's a common sight so there's no point". The constable does not explain himself very well, but his testimony dovetails with evidence obtained from the survey of public attitudes.

Source: Banton, *The Times Higher Education Supplement*, 13 January, 1984 (extract from a review of Smith *et al*, *Police and People in London,* Policy Studies Institute, 1983).

☐ 1 **Describe the *effects* of labelling. What are the *origins* of the labelling process?**
2 **Take any other group of your choice— teachers, nurses, social security clerks, social workers. Devise a method of studying how these groups label their 'clients'. See if you can carry out this research—What are:**
the origins?
the effects?

Mental illness

One of the areas in which labelling theory has been most productive is in its analysis of mental illness and its treatment. It arose as a critique of the traditional positivistic psychiatric model of mental illness which is the most commonly used approach to understanding the phenomenon of mental illness.

According to this model, certain people who exhibit signs of bizarre behaviour are, in fact, suffering from a form of clearly distinguishable illness which is caused by:

disturbing experiences which have usually occurred in childhood and which have distorted the normal process of development. This is the *psychoanalytic* approach. Here the cure is generally to allow the person to bring the memory of the disturbing experiences from the subconscious to the conscious and then to help the 'patient' to conquer the problem;

a reflection of some *physical problem* which is affecting the correct biological functioning of the brain. The 'cure' here is some form of surgery on the brain—locotomy or lobotomy or control of the 'disease' by mind-altering drugs.

In practice, control of mental illness in Britain is usually through the use of drugs which are routinely used to control mental states. For example, at any one time 20 per cent of women in Britain are taking some form of behaviour-altering drug, and 10 per cent of men.

The labelling perspective

Labelling theorists present a serious challenge to conventional approaches in two ways. First, they claim that mental illness is a label that is applied to the behaviour of certain people (and, therefore, not others) in certain circumstances, and no more. The mentally ill, at least initially, are little different from 'normal', it is just that they have had the label 'mentally ill' attached to their behaviour, and this has consequences for their self-perception and for how other people treat them.

Second, the very concept of mental illness is socially constructed. What is considered to be bizarre or inexplicable behaviour varies according to circumstance. It is not that certain forms of behaviour are intrinsically 'mad', rather that our definition of what is normal (and therefore abnormal or insane) varies over time and between different people.

A simple example of how we change our definitions of mental illness over time concerns the Victorian 'illness' of *hysteria*, a form of neurosis. This was regarded as a major female problem at the time, with women exhibiting physical symptoms which had no clear medical causes. Today, this is no longer the case, probably because behaviour which was effectively prohibited for women in the last century is today regarded as perfectly normal. The sheer frustration of the narrow, controlled lives of intelligent women may have exhibited itself in the symptoms of 'hysteria'. Today, one of the major 'mental illnesses' which hits women is *clinical depression*, yet there appears to be little evidence that this was considered a problem one hundred years ago. Mental illness has become a category into which we consign all forms of behaviour which make no sense to us. If an action can not be explained in orthodox terms or with some 'normal' mitigating circumstances, such as drunkenness or the influence of drugs, then we may classify the act as mentally disturbed, depending upon who it is and the circumstances of the action.

☐ **There are numerous examples of how the definition of behaviour varies according to variations in who commits the act, when an act is committed and the circumstances surrounding the act.**

Using the variables suggested (see p. 55–56), give examples of how acts are defined in one situation as normal and in the other as evidence of mental instability.

The concept of mental illness

One of the foremost writers on mental illness is Thomas Scheff who argues there is no such thing as mental illness as such, rather that it is a dustbin category into which we chuck all 'bizarre' behaviour that cannot be explained through the use of alcohol or drug use. It is not that some people are 'ill', rather their behaviour does not make sense to us.

Scheff claims that most people pass through stages of depression or 'acting oddly', but that in the majority of cases other people do not label that behaviour as signs of mental illness. Terms like 'she's a bit depressed at the moment', or 'he's not like himself at the moment', followed by a simple explanation such as 'he/she's got a lot on his/her mind' are typical.

Lemert's concept of primary and secondary deviance, which we discussed earlier, is useful here. The initial acts are of little importance, what is important is if certain of the acts become labelled as evidence of mental illness—it is at this point that important consequences may follow.

A third element of Scheff's argument is that a 'stereotyped imagery of mental illness is learned in early childhood and continually reaffirmed, inadvertently, in ordinary social interaction'. The way in which we view mental illness and respond to it is a result of stereotypes which we learn in the socialisation process. Terms like 'she's gone mad', 'he's acting like a lunatic' are commonly-used phrases. To strengthen these images the media portrayal of mental illness usually consists of showing psychopaths with staring eyes and manic behaviour. A study by Nunnaly showed that the media had 'adopted a stylized picture of mental health problems which distorts reality, but is a useful device in drama, comedy and other programmes for the public'. According to Scheff, the implication for this learning process is that people may well be influenced by these stereotypes in their recognition of mental illness. Even more importantly, if someone does accept the label of being mentally ill, then they seek out a model for their behaviour and this can be found in the stereotypes. People labelled mentally ill, therefore, model their own behaviour on the stereotypes of mental illness learned through the media and in childhood.

The 'career' of the mental patient

According to Scheff, the definition of mental illness and people's responses to it are related to social processes. However:

a) why are some people labelled as mentally ill and others not;
b) what are the consequences of being labelled?

Goffman has suggested that an answer to these questions can be provided by using the concept of a 'career'. This is the process of a person being defined as mentally ill and then learning to redefine him/herself as a 'mentally ill person' who needs help. The career begins with the labelling of a person as mentally ill and then through the influence of professionals in the field, the person comes to accept this definition of him/herself. At the time Goffman was writing, the person defined as mentally ill was likely to be placed in an institution. Incarceration in a mental institution was claimed to have further consequences for the individual and to actually harm the possibilities of re-entering the community. In Britain today however, entry into mental institutions is rare and the emphasis is strongly on 'community care', so we should beware in accepting Goffman's arguments too uncritically for Britain.

Why are some people labelled?

Goffman suggests that it is not the behaviour exhibited by a person, as much as how others respond to exhibited behaviour. The process of labelling usually begins because it is in someone's interest to do so. For example the eccentric grandfather now suffers from dementia because his room is needed for the children, or the wife is now suffering from clinical depression, because the husband is sick of looking after her and has formed another relationship anyway.

An example of this is given in Laing and Esterton's study of schizophrenia, *Sanity, Madness and the Family*. This consists of a number of detailed studies of the family life of diagnosed schizophrenics. In the story of the Abbots, the daughter Maya had entered hospital as a voluntary patient with paranoid schizophrenia, where she had remained for ten years. The initial approach to the Social Services for help had come from her parents who complained that she thought they were conspiring against her, that she threatened to poison her father, and that she was completely withdrawn. When Laing and Esterton investigated the home life and relationships between the parents and daughter they found that the actions of the daughter were perfectly understandable. The parents had failed to come to terms with the inevitable process of their daughter's growing-up and the fact that this involved her gaining a personality of her own, separate from theirs. They *did* talk behind her back as she claimed and they *did* pry into her affairs, refusing her any privacy or even thoughts of her own. The parents had reached a point where the only way they could comprehend the actions of their daughter was to define her as mentally ill. The daughter was hospitalised and labelled a paranoid schizophrenic. In this way, the parents succeeded in restricting their daughter's independence and received official backing for their view of the situation.

The objection most people make to the labelling theorists' approach is that people labelled as mentally ill really do demonstrate the appropriate symptoms. Labelling theorists reply to this by arguing that the 'patients' show the symptoms as a *result* of the labelling process.

To understand this, we need to continue our examination of the concept of 'career'. So far, we have seen that some people are successfully labelled because it is in the interests of others to so do.

Next, we need to find out how the continuing process of labelling and label reinforcement can influence people's *perceptions of themselves*.

The consequences of labelling

Once a person is labelled, then other people tend to engage in *spurious interaction* with them. This term was first used by Erving Goffman. It means that because the doctor, nurse or social worker already knows that the person is mentally ill, then he/she will treat the conversation and actions in this light. In practice, this means reinterpreting or ignoring what the labelled person says. The interaction, therefore, is only one way. Of course, spurious interaction is not restricted solely to dealings with the mentally ill, it also takes place in classrooms, within families and in old people's homes.

Committal into a mental institution. Scheff studied the procedure for involuntary committal into mental institutions in one state in the USA, in particular studying the psychiatric examination which was one element of committal. In order to be committed against one's will, a number of quite strict legal criteria had to be met in the psychiatric examination. However, Scheff concluded that in 66 per cent of cases, these legal criteria were not met. An observer who attended these examinations felt that questions were hurried and pressured and would cause problems for most people in normal circumstances, let alone in the stressful situation of a compulsory medical examination. Even where there was little evidence for committal, the psychiatrist felt it safer to commit the person on the assumption that the 'patient' would not have been brought for examination if there was nothing wrong with them.

> *One examiner (psychiatrist) ... recommended a 30-day observation for a patient whom he had thought* not *to be mentally ill, on the grounds that the patient, a young man, could not get along with his parents and 'might get into trouble'.*

Another physician, after a very short interview (8 minutes), told the observer:

> *On the schizophrenics, I don't bother asking them more questions when I can see they're schizophrenic because* I know what they are going to say. *You could talk to them another half-hour and not learn any more.*

The point this study reinforces is that once a label is applied it is extremely difficult to deny it. Contact with other people will be on the basis that the labelled person is ill and what he/she says can be discounted.

In the institution. The next stage in the career occurs if the person is in an institution, where he/she is treated as labelled even if the 'patient's' behaviour is perfectly normal.

Rosenhan conducted an experiment in which students were admitted to various US mental hospitals by claiming that they were hearing voices. However, once accepted, the students acted perfectly normally and replied to all questions entirely honestly. They were diagnosed as schizophrenics and then treated as if whatever they did or said was evidence of insanity. For example, the researchers would write down their observations in notebooks, as requested by Rosenhan. Later examining the nurse's notes on the 'pseudo patients', Rosenhan discovered the comment that the 'patient manifests writing behaviour'. When they spoke to the staff, the doctors and patients would simply ignore the actual content of the request or statement and make some innocuous or spurious remark. The researchers felt that it was increasingly difficult to behave normally in an environment in which those around did not respond in a normal manner.

Goffman has suggested that this sort of response by staff is part of the wider process of stripping away a person's *presenting culture* and forcing him/her into accepting the definitions of him/herself made by the institution. By 'presenting culture', Goffman means the front we all present to others as our self-image. This consists of our clothes and hair-styles, plus our manner towards others. The definitions of the mental institution usually derive from: a) the assumption the person is mentally ill and therefore has lost the right to make his/her own decisions and; b) that the person ought to be co-operative to the organisational needs of the institution. The patient's self-image, for instance of a witty, well-dressed middle aged man, is stripped away leaving him bewildered and vulnerable, ready to accept the new role allocated to him. Attempts to disrupt or oppose the regime of the hospital are controlled by enforced drug dosages. This treatment is legitimised in the eyes of the staff by the fact that the person is 'mentally ill' and, therefore, his/her viewpoint is not to be taken seriously.

Adapting to institutional life. The activities described above serve to stabilise the patient in the role of someone who is mentally ill. This is reinforced by other factors such as the patient finding a way of adapting to institutional life. Goffman suggests that there are five possible ways in which patients adapt:

> *situational withdrawal*: here the patient simply withdraws into him/herself. This is often taken as evidence of schizophrenia, incidentally.
> *intransigence*: this is where the patient refuses to cooperate and this can lead to a spiral of incidents with the staff, in which they take the patient's refusal to co-operate as evidence of illness and will usually turn to ever stronger drugs in an effort to control the disruptive behaviour.
> *colonisation*: the patient makes him/herself fully at home and does not wish to leave the institution—this is often termed 'institutionalisation', and has become recognised as a major problem when trying to rehabilitate ex-mental patients in the community, as they simply refuse to leave.
> *conversion*: where the patient imitates the actions of the staff and is used by staff for various minor tasks. These are usually classified as 'co-operative'.
> *playing it cool*: this (rather 1960s term!) refers to those who simply concentrate on getting out intact from the institution and play by the rules, without ever fully co-operating.

Life outside the institution. Although Scheff and Goffman's works are extremely interesting, their use is rather limited by the decline in the number of mentally ill patients resident in institutions. Increasingly in Britain the emphasis is on 'community care'. This means in practice that the large mental hospitals are being shut down and the mentally ill are either being treated at home—(in the family which may have helped cause the problem in the first place, according to Laing!)—or they are placed in accommodation and treated in day centres. Today only the more severe cases of mental illness are being treated on a long-term basis as residents. Does the power of labelling exist outside the institution? There is little contemporary research on this, but it is clear that those who are labelled mentally ill who live in the community are treated with considerable caution by the rest of the 'normal' population. Scheff asked a sample of people if they would employ someone who had been mentally ill but was now recovered, as: a) a babysitter or; b) as a taxi driver. The reply to both questions was a resounding *no.* Yet Scheff points out, if asked about a person who had fully recovered from a serious heart complaint the majority of the sample felt little difficulty in trusting them. There is also no reason to suppose the 'normal' population are less likely to engage in spurious interaction than the staff of a mental institution.

Conclusion

The labelling perspective paints an entirely different picture of mental illness than the traditional psychiatric 'medical' model. Labelling stresses the socially created nature of mental illness and the contribution others make to the acquisition of symptoms of illness which occur after the labelling has taken place.

Criticisms of the labelling approach

The labelling approach has been criticised for ignoring the reality of mental illness and for failing to appreciate the very real conditions which lead certain groups to have high rates of mental illness.

Often mental illness derives from a lack of material resources and meaningful relationships, which results in feelings of worthlessness and despair. Mental illness does not hit the population randomly, but is far more likely to strike the poor than the affluent; females, especially housewives, rather than males; blacks rather than whites, and so on.

Mental illness and gender

Brown and Harris (*The Social Origins of Depression*) studied 600 women in South London, and found clear differences between the social classes in the incident of depression (a classic female 'mental problem').

They suggest that there are two clearly distinguishable sets of factors. First, *major life events* (or *provoking agents*); these can be *long-term* eg. poverty or chronic physical ill health, or *unforeseen*, eg. marriage breakdown or the death of a close relative.

Second, *protective and vulnerability factors*: women with strong and supportive relationships can usually overcome the problems caused by the provoking agents, but if there is an absence of these, plus other factors such as having three or more young children, being poor or unemployed, then the women are more likely to suffer depression. *Protective factors* is the term used to describe the situation where supportive relationships (amongst other things) exist. The term *vulnerability factors* refers to the absence of these.

Brown and Harris found that working class women were more likely to have 'provoking agents', and less likely to have 'protective factors'. The result was greater likelihood of clinical depression.

The point of Brown and Harris's study is that certain groups genuinely undergo problems which are more likely to leave them open to certain types of mental illness. However, we can go even deeper than this and see that the *culture* of society can lead to higher rates of mental illness amongst certain groups.

In *Women and Psychiatry* Lipshitz argues that the higher rate of mental illness among women is related to their role in society. She claims that women are expected to be dependent and emotional and illogical, while men are expected to be aggressive and independent. Lipshitz argues that when women step outside this role then they are in danger of being labelled as mentally ill. However, one could argue that men are equally trapped in their sex role, and rather than it being a problem specifically for women, it may be equally true for both sexes.

Mental illness and race

In *Aliens and Alienists*, Littlewood and Lipsedge point out that black people and Asians are twice as likely to be involuntarily detained under the Mental Health Act than whites. When differences in diagnoses are allowed for, they are more likely to receive heavier dosage of the most powerful drugs than whites and to be more likely to receive electro-convulsive therapy.

One explanation for these facts could be that doctors are racist, yet it appears that black patients are more likely to be examined by black psychiatrists. An alternative thesis, put forward by Littlewood and Lipsedge is that the racist nature of British society acts in such a way as to repress blacks and Asians. Living in a society where they are regarded as inferior and where they arc bottom of the ladder in ownership of material goods, they feel cut off from the dominant British society in which they live and powerless to alter their situation. According to the authors, black people are likely to be alienated and in a situation of anomie. The result is that they are more likely to suffer from mental illness, as they struggle to overcome their situation.

The labelling of acts as deviant

We have just examined the way people can be labelled as deviant and seen how that process has important consequences for them. However, any understanding of *why* people come to be labelled as deviant must be related to why some *acts* are considered deviant. After all, a deviant is merely a person who is believed to have committed a deviant act.

Most of us can construct a list of acts which we would argue are deviant in themselves—for example, the killing of another human being. Yet we can also see that in certain circumstances this view changes. The obvious example is the killing that occurs in wartime. So, it is not the act of killing Itself that is bad (or good) but the circumstances in which this takes place.

This *relative* element of morality prompted Becker to argue that there are no such things as actions which are deviant in themselves, merely acts that people define as deviant in certain circumstances.

The labelling perspective centres on two areas. Firstly, what is considered deviant and criminal varies. Secondly, social rules are not fixed and natural, but instead are created by people for various reasons.

According to Becker, there seems little point in studying why people break laws until one understands why the rules exist in the first place.

It is important to note that laws vary according to a number of circumstances, including the following:

☐ **Give your own examples of the variation of deviance according to the headings opposite. Are there any other headings you could suggest?**

Do all people regard the same acts as deviant? Construct a brief attitude questionnaire, then ask different groups of people (for example, divided by occupation, gender, age etc) if they regard the acts as 'bad' or not. What do the results indicate? What does this tell us about the labelling theory?

Who commits the act. For example, if a child gets drunk it is deviant, if an adult, then it is acceptable, and a drunken woman is generally regarded as far worse than a drunken man.

When the act is committed. Twenty years ago, child abuse was generally ignored, today it is regarded as a major evil of society.

The places where acts are committed. Bathing naked in Majorca is different from entering the local swimming pool (un)dressed in a similar way.

The society/culture in which the act takes place. One society may well accept an act which another considers deviant. For instance the emancipation of women in Western societies enables women to do things which in Muslim societies would be labelled deviant.

The historical/political circumstance. For example, the deliberate killing of another person in wartime is good, but in peace it is murder.

If we accept that acts are not good or bad in themselves, but that they are defined as wrong or illegal in a variety of circumstances, then the next stage must be to explain the variation.

The process of rule creation

According to Becker what is considered deviant is neither a reflection of the 'will of the people', as the functionalists claim, nor is it necessarily a reflection of the interests of the ruling class, as the Marxists argue. Instead, Becker claims that individuals or groups set about making certain acts illegal because they see it as in their own interests, or they genuinely believe it to be in the interests of the rest of society.

☐ **Construct a chart with these headings and then break the following 'story' into the relevant sections:**
   the events
   the crime
   normal attitudes to crime
   moral entrepreneur
   the label
   the consequence of the label.

One day an outbreak of wailing and a great commotion told me that a death had occurred somewhere in the neighbourhood. Kima'i, a young lad of my acquaintance, of sixteen or so, had fallen from a coco-nut palm and killed himself.

He had broken the rules of exogamy, (with) the daughter of his mother's sister. This had been known and generally disapproved of but nothing was done until the girl's discarded lover, who had wanted to marry her and who felt personally injured, took the initiative. This rival threatened first to use black magic against the guilty youth, but this had not much effect. Then one evening he insulted the culprit in public accusing him in the hearing of the whole community of incest and hurling at him certain expressions intolerable to a native.

For this there was only one remedy; only one means of escape remained to the unfortunate youth. Next morning he put on festive attire and ornamentation, climbed a coco-nut palm and addressed the community, speaking from among the palm leaves and bidding them farewell. He explained the reasons for his desperate deed and also launched forth a veiled accusation against the man who had driven him to his death, upon which it became the duty of his clansmen to avenge him. Then he wailed aloud, as is the custom, jumped from a palm some sixty feet high and was killed on the spot. There followed a fight within the village in which the rival was wounded; and the quarrel was repeated during the funeral. . .

The Trobrianders show horror at the idea of violating the rules of exogamy and they believe that disease and even death might follow clan incest. This is the ideal of native law, and in moral matters it is easy and pleasant strictly to adhere to the ideal, when judging the conduct of others or expressing an opinion about conduct in general.

When it comes to the application of morality and ideals to real life, however, things take on a different complexion. In the case described it was obvious that the facts would not tally with the ideal of conduct. Public opinion was neither outraged by the knowledge of the crime to any extent, nor did it react directly—it had to be mobilized by a public statement of the crime and by insults being hurled at the culprit by an interested party and even then he had to carry out the punishment himself . . . The breach of exogamy—as regards intercourse and not marriage—is by no means a rare occurrence, and public opinion is lenient, though decidedly hypocritical. If the affair is carried on *sub rosa* with a certain amount of decorum, and if no one in particular stirs up trouble, "public opinion"

will gossip, but not demand any harsh punishment. If, on the contrary, scandal breaks out—everyone turns against the guilty pair and by ostracism and insults one or the other may be driven to suicide.

Whether an act is deviant . . . depends on how other people react to it. You can commit clan incest and suffer from no more than gossip as long as no one makes a public accusation: but you will be driven to your death if the accusation is made. The point is that the response of other people has to be regarded as problematic. Just because one has committed an infraction of a rule does not mean that others will respond as though this had happened. (Conversely, just because one has not violated a rule does not mean that he may not be treated, in some circumstances, as though he had.)

Source: Becker, *Outsiders*, Macmillan, 1963

Becker advances an essentially *pluralist* argument to explain the creation of rules in society, by claiming that interested groups, or as he calls them *moral entrepreneurs*, attain law changes by mobilising enough support to alter social rules.

☐ **Look up the pluralist model of the state in a textbook. Compare the interactionist and pluralist models. Do any clear conclusions emerge?**

☐ **. . . 'social groups create deviance by making the rules whose infraction constitutes deviance' (*Outsiders*, H. S. Becker).**
   What are the implications of Becker's statement for the study of deviance?
   What comments would:
      functionalists
      Marxists
      subcultural theorists
      positivist theorists
   make on this quote?
   Could you suggest any acts which are intrinsically deviant?

Labelling in practice

The rest of this chapter will be devoted to showing how the relatively simple ideas of labelling can be applied to areas such as mental illness, the role of the media and the police, and the process of law making. The effect is to provide a very different analysis to other sociological approaches.

The process of law creation

As we have just seen, labelling theory provides us with considerable insight into how the individual is affected by being defined as a criminal, or mentally ill. But labelling theory goes beyond this and argues that rule creation is the result of a labelling process too. I have chosen two examples which will explain this model of law creation. Firstly, the development of laws in the United States against marihuana use and secondly, the origins of the juvenile courts there.

The Marihuana Tax Act

Until 1937 smoking marihuana was legal in the United States, even though opiates had been banned for a considerable time before that.

Becker suggests that underlying the ban on drugs are three American values:

1. *The Protestant value of self control and responsibility.* In Protestant-based societies there is considerable stress placed on the fact that people make decisions on the basis of rational choice, and should then accept the responsibility for the consequences of the original decision. Drugs distort this relationship, as people are not in full self-control when they commit acts—therefore, are they actually responsible for their acts?
2. *Disapproval of states of ecstasy.* In American culture, the idea of 'states of ecstasy' provokes feelings of unease, even in a religious context. The idea of achieving these states through drugs is seen as wrong, and an example of the search for selfish pleasure.
3. *Humanitarianism.* Anything which enslaves people, depriving them of their right to free choice is seen as abhorrent. Drugs (and alcohol) do just that and, therefore, stand condemned.

The result of these three values had been the banning of alcohol, during the period of Prohibition and the Harrison Act (1937) which banned the use of opiates except for approved medical purposes.

The moral entrepreneurs

However, the existence of values does not lead to the passage of legislation. What are needed are *moral entrepreneurs* to wage a *moral crusade* on behalf of the enforcement of the values in a specific context. In this case it was the Treasury Department's Bureau of Narcotics that launched the moral crusade. Becker suggests that the motives that led them to do so were:

> ... *that they perceived an area of wrongdoing that properly belonged in their jurisdiction and moved to put it there. The personal interest they satisfied in pressing for marihuana legislation was one common to many officials: the interest in successfully accomplishing the task one has been assigned and in acquiring the best tools with which to accomplish it.*

Here Becker is explaining that, as the Bureau was already responsible for opiates, the extension into marihuana seemed a sensible step to the officials in the bureaucracy.

The moral crusade

Moral crusades, according to Becker, usually involve enlisting the support of other interested organisations and developing a favourable public attitude towards the proposed rule. The first part of this strategy was to win over another powerful branch of the federal bureaucracy, the National Conference of Commissioners on Uniform State Laws, which attempted to co-ordinate the implementation of laws in the various US States (American States have the right to create their own legislation within certain constitutional limits). When there was some delay in assistance from the National Conference, the Bureau of Narcotics imposed some inter-bureaucratic 'blackmail' on it, by threatening to by-pass it. This posed a threat for the prestige and power of the National Conference, so they agreed to fully support the Bureau.

When it came to winning over the public, the Bureau ran a long campaign, releasing selected information to the press concerning the terrible effects of marihuana, which *sensitised* the public to the issue of marihuana use and helped to create a strong climate of opinion in favour of legislation. Here is an extract of a magazine article based on information provided by the Bureau.

> *An entire family was murdered by a youthful (marihuana) addict in Florida. When officers arrived at the home they found the youth staggering about in a human slaughterhouse. With an axe he had killed his father, mother, two brothers and a sister. He seemed to be in a daze ... He had no recollection of having committed the multiple crime. The officers knew him ordinarily as a sane, rather quiet young man; now he was pitifully crazed. They sought the reason. The boy said he had been in the habit of smoking something which youthful friends called 'muggles', a childish name for marihuana.* (Quoted in Becker Outsiders, p.142)

The campaign started in 1932 and by 1937 the Congress began to consider a bill, outlawing the sale and use of marihuana.

The issue of power

The only opposition came from manufacturers of hempseed oil, who argued that they used the marihuana seed as an essential element of their manufacturing process. After some discussion with the organised hempseed lobby, the government modified its bill to allow its continuing use by the manufacturers, as long as the seed was sterilised. Marihuana smokers, as an unorganised group, had no say. In July 1937, the Act was passed.

The child savers

Much of the content of labelling theory centres around the view that how people define deviants and respond to them is less a result of the act they have committed, than of other factors. A good example of this is the way we treat young people who commit theft. Instead of treating them as criminals who need punishment, they are (at least initially) treated as young delinquents who need help and treatment.

The origins of special courts and penal institutions for youth in late nineteenth century USA was the subject of Platt's study, as he wished to find out just why they developed at that particular time.

Background values

Underlying the whole debate on delinquency and crime were two values which had a tremendous influence on thinkers during this period:

Nature versus nurture debate. The traditional idea that criminals were 'born bad' was giving way to the newer explanations of psychology and sociology. In particular, the belief was growing that people were 'made bad', or corrupted by bad family or peer group influences. This theme is still common in much writing on juvenile crime.

Urban disenchantment. There was a growing dislike of the huge US cities with their high levels of crime, poverty and slum districts. Middle class commentators argued that many of the social problems were a direct result of city life. If only people could be removed from its corrupting influences then the social problems might be overcome.

These two values led many reformers to the belief that if they could only take young offenders out of the cities to the countryside, where they could be put in reformatories and set to work in the clean, pure outdoors, away from the corrupting influence of city, peer group and family, they would learn to become 'good' people.

The moral entrepreneurs

Platt points out the tremendous influence of women on the development of the juvenile justice system and explains this by referring to the way that middle and upper class women had been edged out of any major employment role at that period. Their role was to run the household for their husbands and family. Clearly this left large numbers of intelligent, articulate women unfulfilled. The outlets for their energies were rather limited, but one possibility lay in charity work, and within this field the most 'appropriate' area for a woman was to work with children.

Although the women were generally motivated to help young people, there were advantages for them as a result of their campaign. Most importantly:

> ... it had ... considerable practical significance for legitimizing new career openings for women. The new role of social worker combined elements of an old and partly fictitious role—defenders of family life—and elements of a new role—social servant. Social work was thus both an affirmation of cherished American values and an instrument for women's emancipation.

Source: Platt, 'The Rise of the Child Saving Movement', *Annals of the American Academy,* January 1969

The moral crusade

The women pursued their campaign with some vigour, lobbying at all levels of the legislature. However, their most powerful weapons were their husbands who were generally well-connected in business and politics. It was through them that the reform movement channelled their pressure. The result was a new system of justice for youth, who were tried in separate juvenile courts, and then sent to separate penal institutions in order to reform rather than punish them.

☐ **PROJECT**

Using the headings of *Values, Moral entrepreneurs, Moral crusade*, investigate the passage of one bill (successful or not) through parliament. One interesting example is the Alton Abortion Bill, February 1988.

Conclusion

The examples examined above show that labelling theory provides a very clear model of law creation based on the concept of a moral crusade waged by moral entrepreneurs. Most rules, formal or informal, follow this pattern. This model is, as Becker says:

> *... equally applicable not only to legislation in general, but to the development of rules of a more informal kind. Wherever rules are created and applied, we should be alive to the possible presence of an enterprising individual or group ... Whenever rules are created and applied we should expect to find people attempting to enlist the support of coordinate groups and using the available media of communication to develop a favourable climate of opinion, where they do not develop such support, we may expect to find their enterprise unsuccessful.*

Source: Becker, *Outsiders,* Macmillan, 1963

'When I brought in Bill C-51, I said this was going to be war. The tobacco companies were not in the business of losing battles, and they hadn't lost a lot of battles throughout the history of the industry.' — Canadian Health Minister Jake Epp.

It is war—and the tobacco industry is losing it. The industry fears the Bill will convert it from a multi-billion-dollar-a-year economic dynamo into a faltering cottage industry.

Under the pending law, tobacco ads will be banned from Canadian newspapers after the Bill passes later this month. On January 1, 1989, all tobacco ads on billboards and in magazines, and sponsorship of televised or non-televised sports and cultural events, must stop.

There are no ads for tobacco products on Canadian TV or radio because, in 1972, the industry 'volunteered' to stay off the air to avoid a government-imposed ban. That was the tobacco industry's one concession to the federal government in the last great battle over advertising.

The industry won that round, but now it's certain to lose, despite a threat to launch a court challenge on the grounds that the ad ban violates the constitutional right to freedom of expression.

The Canadian Daily Newspaper Publishers Association has also denounced the ad ban as a blow to free speech. One publisher, ignoring charges that he was concerned about lost revenue, said: "The principle bothers us."

Another said the ban creates a dangerous precedent by outlawing the advertising of a legal product. But several newspapers which oppose the ban have voluntarily removed tobacco ads from their pages.

The Health Minister rejects the pro-tobacco claim of constitutionally-guaranteed freedom to advertise. "The responsible exercise of freedom of speech does not include the freedom to portray a lethal product as glamorous or socially-acceptable," he said.

The advertising industry says it will lose as much as $75 million under the ban. And at one press conference, the chain-smoking chairman of the Canadian Tobacco Manufacturers Association, warned that 2,500 advertising employees will lose their jobs.

But the Bill before the House of Commons is assured of speedy passage because it has almost unanimous support.

Mr Epp introduced the legislation because the tobacco advertisers had begun to concentrate on attracting new smokers by depicting young people in 'lifestyle' activities—sailing, skiiing, socialising.

Opposition MP Lynn McDonald, a supporter of the Bill and an anti-tobacco crusader, said: "We know why the tobacco companies have to advertise—because 35,000 Canadians a year are dying (of tobacco-related diseases). They are the customers of these companies. Some 350,000 smokers, largely intelligent, adult men, are quitting smoking. The tobacco companies have to replace their customers."

The tobacco companies thought they had leverage over the government through their sponsorships of sports and cultural events.

The government's bill allows the tobacco company to be named as a supporter, but not its cigarette brand names.

The tobacco companies have threatened to withdraw sponsorship, saying they don't sell their corporate names, they sell cigarette brands.

The Cancer Society is pleased. A spokesman said the tobacco companies have always used their sponsorship of special events for no other reason than "to buy respectability."—Reuter

Source: Benesh, 'Burnt fingers in tobacco row', *The Guardian*, 9 February, 1988

□ 1 Three approaches:
(a) Marxists criticise labelling theory for its inability to present a coherent argument on the way laws are created; (b) Labelling theorists suggest a 'pluralist' or 'pressure-group' model of law making; (c) Marxists suggest a 'ruling-class' model.
Which approach does the last newspaper report support?

2 Construct a chart comparing the main factors of the Marxist and Labelling approaches. Is there any way that a researcher could substantiate one or other of the two approaches?

Crime and the media

In the Becker extract, you may have noticed the importance he places on the use of 'the available media of communication' in running a successful moral crusade.

Labelling theorists have been particularly interested in the role of the media and crime, and have pointed in particular to two processes of *sensitisation* and *deviancy amplification* which they associate with the media. This particular element of labelling theory has been very influential in sociology and has influenced thinking in other perspectives, such as Marxism. In this section, the importance of the media will be explored.

Deviancy amplification and the media

The best known (and probably still the best!) study of deviancy amplification and the media is S. Cohen's *Folk Devils and Moral Panics*. Cohen studied the fighting between the Mods and Rockers in 1964. Mods can reasonably be seen as the originals of such diverse groups as skinheads and 'casuals' of the 1970s/early 1980s. They were distinguishable by their taste for soul music, 'Parka' ex-army coats and motor scooters. The 'Rockers' were the original 'Bikers'. They wore leather jackets, rode motor bikes and listened to rock and roll. During Easter Sunday 1964, some spasmodic and isolated incidents of fighting broke out among bored youths in the coastal resort of Clacton. The fights were neither serious nor noteworthy but they resulted in twenty-four youths being arrested. Coinciding with these innocuous events, however, journalists on national newspapers found themselves short of hard 'news' material and exaggerated and distorted what had occurred. The newspapers stressed that violence was caused by clearly identifiable groups of Mods and Rockers, who hated each other and had gone to Clacton deliberately to cause trouble. Feature articles contained interviews with Mods and Rockers and discussions of their lifestyles. Yet Cohen comments that before the media coverage, although divisions between Mods and Rockers existed, they were weak and of little significance to the youths themselves. After the coverage however, British youth polarised sharply into those associating themselves with either the Mods or the Rockers.

During the following Whitsun Bank Holiday, the newspapers predicted scenes of blood and violence in certain 'target' towns. Although the Mods and Rockers (and other youth) turned up in large numbers, they mainly milled around uncertain of exactly what they were supposed to do. Nevertheless, newspapers still managed to create headlines suggesting excitement and violence.

The newspaper predictions influenced the police and magistrates too, and the police were strongly reinforced to deal with the violence. As the police had been 'sensitised' by the press, they reacted at the slightest hint of trouble. The result was that more people than usual were arrested—not necessarily because there was significantly more trouble, but because they were more likely than usual to arrest youths who seemed to fit the stereotype of Mod or Rocker. This process of sensitisation also affected the magistrates who imposed heavier penalties than normal in order to combat the crime wave. According to Cohen, this was a process by which the media actually created crime, through its exaggeration and distortion. Cohen used the term *deviancy amplification* to describe this process. The distortion of events and the labelling by the media of a group of youths as troublemakers (*folk devils*), created the stereotyped image held by police officers and the public, which led them to respond forcibly against the perceived threat to law and order (*a moral panic*).

Deviancy amplification and the media

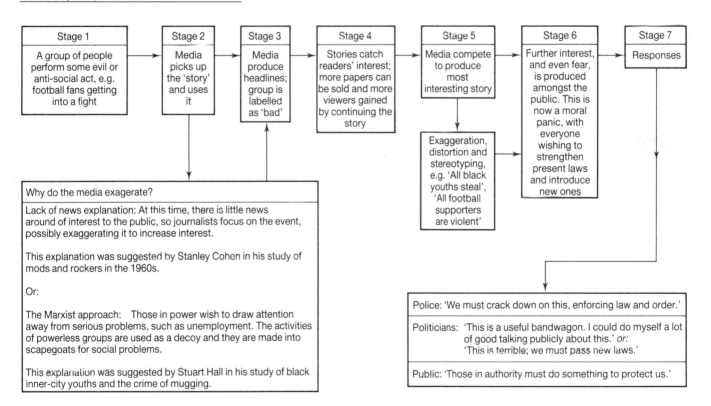

Source: Moore, *Sociology Alive!*, Stanley Thornes, 1987

Crime waves

☐ **Use the model as a guide to analyse a recent event in the news.**

Is the above situation typical of crime reporting in general? The answer appears to be *yes*. Studies indicate that the amount of crime being reported in the newspapers does not indicate the extent of real crime, but is a reflection of other factors.

In *City Politics and Deviance Amplification*, Armstrong and Wilson studied the relationship between crime reporting and the actual amount of crime in Glasgow. They concluded that crime had become a local election issue, and local newspapers devoted large amounts of space to juvenile crime as a means of supporting Conservative political candidates and discrediting the Labour-controlled council. Therefore, this factor was more important in the newspapers' reporting of crime than the real amount of crime.

In 'Crime Waves as Ideology' (from *The Manufacture of News*, by Cohen and Young), Fishman examined an apparent crime wave in New York which consisted of muggings on elderly people. At the height of the media's reporting of this crime wave, the actual amount of mugging of the elderly was *decreasing.*

Firstly, Fishman points out that the crime wave rose and fell depending upon other major stories. If there was a particularly newsworthy non-crime event, then the reporting of muggings would decline. When other events were thin on the ground, the crime wave built up again.

Secondly, Fishman argues that editors are daily faced with a wide range of very disparate items of information which they need to weld together into some form of cohesive news. As a result, editors search for 'themes' which will act as an umbrella for news items to be drawn together under. The theme of street crime allowed a wide range of stories about crime, the police, politicians and elderly people to be welded together into some coherent sets of stories. The result was an apparent crime wave.

The crime wave exists across the media because all the media feed off one another. Newspaper editors and television news editors check the news output of all other media to 'steal' information and stories. As a result, media reporting tends to have similar contents.

□ **Examine the concept of 'newsworthiness', which journalists use to choose certain 'happenings' as news and to ignore others. There is a full discussion of this in chapter 5 of Paul Trowler's** *Investigating the Media.* **How does the concept of 'newsworthiness' help us to understand crime reporting?**

Newspapers' sources

In *Law and Order News*, Chibnall examined how crime reporters actually obtain the information that eventually comprises the news. Firstly, he points out that newspapers do not always reflect the full range of crime, but a combination of what the reporter considers interesting news and what the police are prepared to divulge.

Both these factors mean that most white-collar crime and corporate crime is ignored because the police feel that this is not in their area of responsibility. Also, marital violence, routine theft and shoplifting are generally regarded as unimportant by the police and dull by the crime reporters.

The material that does emerge is generally what is normally regarded as (exciting) material by the reporters and 'real' crime by the police—these include serious crimes such as bank robbery, murder and rape.

These crimes are, therefore, brought to the attention of the crime reporters by the police who are also usually the only available source of information. Hence, the output of the press could be regarded as a reflection of police attitudes and priorities.

A group working at the Centre for Contemporary Cultural Studies push this position even further in discussing definitions of crime.

What in fact we are dealing with is the relation between three different *definitions* of crime: the *official*, the *media* and the *public* definitions of crime. Each of these definitions is socially constructed—a social event not a fact in Nature; each is produced by a distinctive social and institutional process. The *official* definition of crime is constructed by those agencies responsible for crime control—the police, the courts, the statisticians, the Home Office. This definition is the result of the rate of reported crime, the clear-up rate, the focused and organised police response to certain crimes, the way the patterns and rates of crime are interpreted by judges and official spokesmen in the crime control institutions and so on. The *media* definition of crime is constructed by the media, and reflects the selective attention of news men and news media to crime, the shaping power of 'news values', the routines and practices of news gathering and presentation. The *public* definition of crime is constructed by the lay public with little or no direct experience or 'expert' knowledge of crime. It is massively dependent on the other two definitions— the official and the media definitions. The selective portrayal of crime in the mass media plays an important part in shaping public definitions of the 'crime problem', and hence also (through further feed-back) in its 'official' definition. So we must replace the simple equation, crime = apprehension = news about crime with a more complex model, which takes full account of the shaping power of the intervening institutions. Thus:

crime (volume & incidence unknown)

⬇

'crime' (product of institutional definition by crime control agencies)

⬇

news values (the selective institutional practices of 'news making')

⬇

'crime-as-news' (the selective portrayal of crime in the media)

⬇

public definition of crime (the consequence of information provided by official and media sources)

Source: Cohen and Young, *The Manufacture of News,* Constable, 1981

☐ **Construct a detailed diagram showing the factors influencing the way crime is reported.**

Criticisms of the labelling approach

The first criticism of labelling theory is that it fails to explain why people commit crime in the first place! Labelling theorists suggest that all of us commit criminal acts, but only a few of us are caught. This is partially true. Many people have at some time, broken the law—for example, driving over the speed limit, 'stealing' free phone calls at work, etc—but virtually all research has shown that there are significant differences in the likelihood of certain groups of people committing crime than others. In reply, the British interactionist Ken Plummer has argued that labelling theory does not *claim* to explain different rates of crime, nor does it say that everybody breaks the law equally. Instead it examines the importance of *some* of those people being labelled as criminal in terms of how they are treated and how they perceive themselves.

A second criticism is that Becker and Lemert seem to suggest that people who commit crime but are not labelled are, in some sense, not deviant, and there are no consequences for their view of themselves. Furthermore, people are aware that they are committing deviant acts, and the knowledge they can do so without getting caught or labelled can influence their future behaviour. Becker has accepted this criticism, but as he and Plummer point out, the very real consequences of having a deviant label attached to a person remain.

A criticism which Taylor, Walton and Young put forward in their Marxist critique of labelling (see *The New Criminology*) is that it offers no adequate explanation of the role of power in the creation (and enforcement) of criminal laws. Plummer robustly rejects this, pointing out that labelling theory does have a clear model of law creation. This model may not be a Marxist one, but the whole concept of moral entrepreneurs opened up, for the first time, a realisation that laws were the result of the actions of power groupings.

A further problem raised by Taylor, Walton and Young was the failure of labelling theory to link deviance to the (capitalist) structure of society. This is a correct criticism, but then if labelling theory did that, it would simply be a variation of Marxism. Indeed, contemporary Marxist writings on deviance, particularly *left realism* owe a considerable debt to labelling theory.

☐ ESSAYS

1 **Labelling 'theory' has been one of the most influential approaches in sociology. Critically examine the underlying *theory*, referring to studies and writers where appropriate.**
2 **How does labelling theory help us to understand law creation and enforcement?**
3 **Mental illness can be seen as a 'disease' or a 'label'. Examine the different approaches to mental illness. In your answer point out the different implications for 'treatment' of the mentally ill.**
4 **Explain the concept of the career. In what ways does it help us to understand deviance? Illustrate your answer with reference to any *two* areas of social life.**
5 **Examine the relationship between the media and crime.**

Bibliography

H. Becker, *The Outsiders*, Macmillan, 1963

E. Lemert, *Human Deviance, Social Problems and Social Control*, Prentice-Hall, 1972

S. Box, *Deviance, Reality and Society*, Holt, Rinehart and Winston, 1981

J. Kitsuse, *Societal Reaction to Deviant Behaviour*, Social Problems Journal, 1962

T. Scheff, *The role of the mentally ill and the dynamics of mental disorder* in S. Spitzer and N. Denzin (eds), *The Mental Patient*, McGraw-Hill, 1968

E. Goffman, *Asylums*, Penguin, 1968

R. Laing and A. Esterton, *Sanity, Madness and the Family*, Penguin, 1970

D. Rosenhan, *On being sane in insane places*, in Science Journal, volume 179

G. Brown and T. Harris, *The Social Origins of Depression*, Tavistock, 1978

S. Lipshitz, *Women and Psychiatry* in J. Chetwynd and O. Hartnett, *The Sex Role System*, Routledge, 1978

R. Littlewood and M. Lipsedge, *Aliens and Alienists*, Penguin, 1982

J. Platt, *The Rise of the Child Saving Movement*, Annals of the American Academy, January, 1969

S. Cohen, *Folk Devils and Moral Panics*, MacGibbon and Kee, 1972

G. Armstrong and M. Wilson, *City Politics and Deviance Amplification* in *Politics and Deviance* by I. Taylor and L. Taylor, Penguin, 1973

P. Trowler, *Investigating the Media*, Unwin Hyman, 1988

S. Chibnall, *Law and Order News*, Tavistock, 1977

I. Taylor, P. Walton and J. Young, *The New Criminology*, RKP, 1973

D. Campbell, *'Evil Beyond Belief'*, The New Statesman, 6 June, 1986

5 · Marxist Perspectives

Marxist approaches

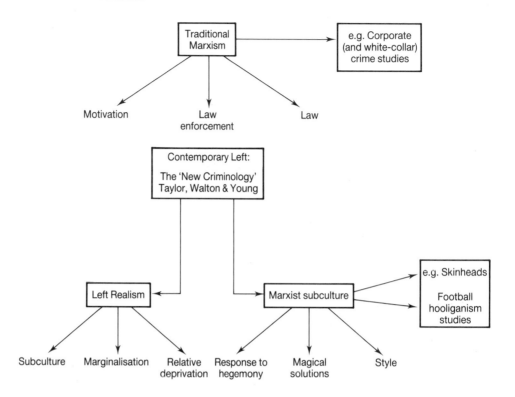

Marxism has been one of the most influential perspectives in sociology. In relation to crime and deviance, however, little was written using the theoretical perspective of Marxism until the 1960s. Since then, there has been a blossoming of work using this approach. In this chapter, and the following related chapters three phases of the Marxist (or *neo-Marxist*) approach will be studied.

Traditional Marxism focuses on the nature of law creation and enforcement, using the theoretical tools that had been developed by Marxists over eighty years. Within this approach there are also discussions on white-collar crime and mugging to illustrate the range of topics covered by the 'traditional Marxists'.

The second element of this approach is *Marxist subculture.* The principal feature of this is youth culture, mainly because most crime in Britain is committed by young people and without an understanding of their motivation it is difficult to see how one can tackle crime and deviance. This approach considerably refined the tools of Marxist analysis and really pulled Marxism in a new direction. Included in this section is a discussion of football hooliganism. This provides an example of how this approach tackles an issue which has caused considerable concern in recent years.

The final Marxist-derived approach covered is *left realism.* This is currently the most influential sociological approach in understanding crime and deviance.

The traditional Marxist approach

The traditional Marxist approach to crime and deviance has focused on the following four areas, which will be used as a framework for discussion:

the manipulation of the basic values and morality of a society,
the process of law creation,
the enforcement of law,
individual motivation.

The term *Marxist* is a much abused one in sociology. The term is used to pull together a wide variety of sociologists, all of whom interpret Marx in different ways and whose sociological and political debts to him vary enormously. In this chapter, as elsewhere in sociological writing, a very broad school of thought has been summarised under the heading of Marxism. This is particularly important because Marx himself had very little to say about crime, merely seeing it as a product of poverty.

The manipulation of values

□ **To understand just how this process of the promotion of capitalist values occurs, look up the Marxist perspectives on the media and education. Look particularly at the work of Althusser, Bowles and Gintis on education, and the Glasgow Media Group's *Bad News* series. (See the Bibliography at the end of this chapter.)**

How do these relate to the discussion of crime?

Marxists see society as dominated and controlled by those who own the 'commanding heights' of industry, commerce and finance. Control is maintained in two distinct but linked ways, through *socialisation* and through *threat*.

In the socialisation process, people are persuaded from childhood onward of the naturalness and worth of the capitalist system. This process involves a wide range of 'agencies', of which the most important are the school and the mass media. These promote the values of 'freedom', of self-interest, of the need to compete and the rights of private property. The result is a society in which the basic values guiding action support the capitalist political and economic system.

Threat is a fallback if the power of socialisation fails ... and so far in Britain it has rarely been used this century. The clearest examples are the current 'troubles' in Northern Ireland and the alleged use of the police as a form of para-military strike-breaking force during the 1984–5 miners' strike. In both situations, sections of the population have proved real threats to the authority of the State and been confronted by the military or the police.

Marxists argue that the definition of what is criminal, therefore, reflects these values. Causing the death of another person while in a fit of temper, for example a husband killing his wife, is regarded as murder. However, the death of factory workers through the use of dangerous chemicals or asbestos in their work environment, when the management *know* the risks involved, is considered at worst as worthy of a fine.

One result of this ideological manipulation of society is that the law is only applied to the less-powerful such as the young, the working class and blacks. So, the less-powerful people are more likely to be arrested, convicted and sentenced to prison, even though the damage and injury they cause may well be less than that of the more-powerful. There is a discussion of Box's work on white-collar and corporate crime later, on pages 73–75.

A further effect of the socialisation process, according to the Marxist view, is to create the belief that criminals are most likely to be drawn from the working class, the young and the black community, living in inner city areas. An important consequence is that there are far more police in inner city areas, who concentrate their efforts on these groups.

A second result is that explanations of crime start with the assumption that criminality is highest amongst the less-powerful groups in society and, therefore, the *causes* of crime are looked for in the shared characteristics of these groups—their culture, their upbringing, their housing patterns etc. This ignores the fact that very similar actions are being performed by the most powerful groups in society, yet these are not defined as criminal.

Law creation

□ **Using Trowler's *Investigating the Media*, analyse how the process of 'setting the agenda' occurs in the media. Do a content analysis of your own on the media over a short period on the agenda towards crime. How would you describe the dominant 'agenda'? How can the idea of 'setting the agenda' be applied to other areas, such as the current debates on education, the health service and the role of the trade unions?**

You will recall Durkheim argued that law is a reflection of the will of the *people*. Marxists totally reject this, for them law is a reflection of the will of the *powerful*. This may not always be apparent immediately, but ultimately it is so.

Marxists argue that, as economic power guarantees political and social power, the rich are able to manipulate the rest of us and pass laws which benefit them. There are basically two ways in which the 'ruling class' ensure that laws which favour them are passed.

First, the manipulation of values described above ensures that the debate on law and order is conducted within a framework based on values sympathetic to the ruling class—this is known as *setting the agenda* (there is an interesting discussion of this in Trowler's *Investigating the Media*, Chapter 7). A simple example of this is the strict controls on picketing and striking which have been introduced in the last few years. The argument is based on the assumption that strikes are somehow 'bad for the country'. It is the '*national interest*' which is threatened by strikers, rather than the *interests of the employers*. The result is that the law is used to help the employers break the strike.

A second method of ensuring that the ruling class have their way is through the use of pressure group activity. Law changes are generally the result of the activities of pressure groups which lobby the government. The most visible of these are organised pressure groups such as the Child Poverty Action Group, which carry out their activities in public. Marxists, however, point to the power of the City of London and its ability to lobby the government in informal ways behind the scenes. There is little publicity, but great influence.

Not all laws, however, are seen to be entirely for the benefit of the ruling class. Clearly, many laws do genuinely protect ordinary people—obvious ones would be the laws on rape, drunken driving, and laws concerning protective machinery in factories. So, genuine concessions can be gained when either the interest of the powerful and the ordinary people overlap, or when representative pressure groups are able to push through genuine reforms to benefit the interests of the wider population.

Finally, there are other occasions when the law does not obviously reflect the will of the powerful, most notably when there are divisions *between* members of the ruling class.

Law enforcement

The further focus of Marxist analysis concerns the different ways that the law is enforced.

Firstly, Marxists would argue that certain *types* of crime are likely to be enforced more rigorously than others. For example, 'street crimes' such as assault and theft are far more likely to be pursued by the police than much 'white-collar' crime, such as fraud or 'insider trading' in the

Geoffrey Collier and his former residence, Oldbury Place.

Last Wednesday, the former Morgan Grenfell securities director walked away a free man, nursing only a suspended one-year prison sentence and a £25,000 fine.

Collier does, as Mr Justice Farquaharson pointed out, face other penalties for his illicit trading in the shares of AE—profit £15,000—and Cadbury Schweppes—loss £10,000. Collier's £250,000-a-year job at Morgan has gone; his membership of the Stock Exchange is certain to follow.

It was the prospect of Collier's uncertain financial future which persuaded Mr Justice Farquaharson to take the lenient line and decide against any custodial sentence. Not for Collier the dubious pleasures of Ford Prison's 'gash alley'. Rather, his new, more restrained residence in Sevenoaks.

The Old Bailey sentence may also have been tempered by the fulsome praise offered by prosecution council Robin Auld for Collier's 'co-operation with the investigators'. Suggestions were immediately raised that the leniency of the sentence passed down could only have been due to Collier's

doing a Boesky and singing.

Not so. Collier's co-operation was confined only to admitting his own guilt, not to incriminating others or passing on information of any insider dealing rings.

Source: Pitcher, 'The Quality of Mercy', *The Observer*, 5 July, 1987

☐ 1 **What is meant by the term 'white-collar crime'? Could you distinguish between this and corporate crime?**
2 **What is the typical attitude of the public and the courts to these sorts of crime?**
3 **Could you suggest an explanation for these in terms of: a) a Marxist perspective; b) a labelling theorist's perspective; c) an anomie theorist's perspective?**
4 **How would you, as a sociology student, track down examples of white-collar and corporate crime? Discuss the strengths and weaknesses of the method you choose.**

City. In fact, white-collar crime is less likely to be reported to the police in the first place, as large financial institutions prefer to deal privately with crime by staff by sacking them rather than creating any scandal.

Second, certain *groups* in the population are more likely to be on the receiving end of law enforcement. Inner city areas have many more police on patrol than other areas. As crime is regarded as most common among the working class, the young and blacks, then there is much greater police presence amongst these communities. The view has been expressed that police *attitudes* are considerably different too, with them using a 'confrontational' approach.

Finally, the Marxists point to the differences in sentencing policies when it comes to certain types of crime. Property theft committed during burglary or robbery is punished by long terms of imprisonment. Financial swindles, if they come to court at all, are not regarded as serious and not necessarily punished with prison sentences.

THE METROPOLITAN BOBBY

V. large hat to keep things under

Blind eye (for certain 'internal' matters)

keen eye to spot suspicious (i.e. coloured) characters

Coons? Blacks? Niggers? I hate their guts. But I don't let it affect my work

status symbol of v. little practical meaning

V. fine line between no results at all, and getting caught getting results

Gentle "voluntary statement persuader"

HAVE YOU SEEN THIS MAN...

Prisoner's rights

M.C. B.M. D.P.

Source: The Times Higher Educational Supplement, 13 January, 1984

Individual motivation for crime

The Marxist approach stresses the importance of placing individual actions within a wide framework, but it does not completely neglect the question of why people decide to commit crime.

In capitalist societies, according to the Marxists, the cultural stress is on competition (rather than co-operation) and the acquisition of wealth. The desire for money can lead those who are blocked off from legitimate chances of gaining wealth to turn to criminal methods. Note that this argument is very similar to Merton's version of anomie. The crucial difference between Merton and most Marxist writers is that whereas Merton sees the stress on material success as being an aberration, the Marxists see greed as built into the very nature of capitalist society.

The creation and enforcement of law in action

Having looked at the theory of the Marxist approach to crime and deviance, it may be useful to look at two areas of discussion which bring out many of the Marxist issues. These are 'mugging' and corporate crime.

Mugging

The following is a summary of *Policing the Crisis*, by Hall *et al*, a study of 'mugging' from a Marxist perspective.

In the early 1970s in Britain the 'new' crime of mugging developed, generally defined as a robbery in the street where someone is threatened or harmed. The interesting point is that mugging was brand new—until the 1970s no one had heard of it in Britain. By 1972 the papers were filled with frightening stories of eldery people attacked in the streets and savagely beaten. According to the Home Secretary, there had been a 129 per cent increase in muggings over the previous four years.

There were calls in Parliament and in the media for a strong police presence in the inner city areas and for a tough 'crackdown' on the groups of people most likely to be involved in mugging, with most newspapers implying that the muggers were predominantly young black people.

According to Hall, violent street crime was not a new phenomenon at all in Britain. Indeed it had a long and 'honourable' history, certainly well back into the last century. The great interest in violent street crime in the early 1970s was rather odd too, as violent crime had increased quite steadily, by about 33 per cent in the fifties and mid-sixties, but the rate of increase had halved by the late 1960s and early 1970s, to about 14 per cent (Hall). As interest rose, the problem of street crime was on the decline. A further interesting point is that there was no criminal act of 'mugging' at the time, and there still isn't one today. The nearest legal category is 'assault with intent to rob'. The Home Secretary's figure of a 129 per cent increase was arrived at by adding together a number of different forms of street crime. Hall concluded, therefore, that the 'moral panic' (see pp. 62–64) was not based upon any real increase in crime. The answer for the outcry over mugging had to lie elsewhere.

In the early 1970s, according to Hall, Britain was entering a period of 'crisis', in which there was a massive increase in strikes, Northern Ireland was almost at the stage of civil war and the inner cities were in a state of ferment. The control of ideology over sections of the population seemed to be weakening. This contrasted with the previous twenty years since the end of the Second World War when Britain appeared to be characterised by harmony and economic affluence.

Hall claims that the public outcry over mugging, which was triggered off by newspaper reports, based in their turn on information supplied by the police, served the useful purpose of justifying repressive policing in the inner city areas. It also made the general point that there were subversive groups in society which needed to be confronted by force. The outcome was a greatly increased police force in the inner cities, operating most forcibly against young blacks, and an increasing acceptance by the public of more repressive policing against potential threats to public order. The full force of the stricter forms of policing was seen in the actions of the police in the miners' strike of 1984–5.

The central elements of Hall's approach which distinguish it as Marxist are twofold. First, the focus of attention is the wider society within which the crimes took place, rather than on any attributes of the criminals. Therefore, the approach is *structural.* Indeed there is hardly any discussion of the reasons which would impel young blacks to commit street crime.

Second, crime can be seen as a result of the very nature of capitalism (the crisis) and the need to maintain order. The police are seen as provocateurs, not agents of the law *responding* to offences committed against society.

It is important to point out that Hall does not claim that the police, government and newspapers deliberately conspired to engineer the whole situation of moral panic over the muggings in order to justify increasingly oppressive policing methods, although that was the outcome. The situation arose from a similar perception amongst these groups that 'things were getting out of hand', and mugging happened to be the issue which acted as the catalyst for action.

FLAT CAP FOR PUTTING REVOLUTIONARY NEWSPAPERS UNDER

MOUTH FOR SHOUTING REVOLUTIONARY SLOGANS

IMPLEMENT FOR INDUSTRIAL SABOTAGE

TO HELP FORGET THE MISERIES OF LIFE UNDER CAPITALIST OPPRESSION.

☐ **We saw earlier that there are four focal areas of Marxist analysis. Explain how Hall's study covers the points of:**

> **the manipulation of values,**
> **the creation of law,**
> **the enforcement of law,**
> **individual motivations.**

From library back-copies/microfiche find the newspapers:
> **from 29 May to 18 June 1984 which cover the disturbances during the miners' strike outside the Orgreave Colliery.**
> **for 12 June to 25 June 1986, covering the 'travelling people's' attempts to reach Stonehenge.**
How do you think Marxists would analyse these?

Criticisms

There are a considerable number of criticisms which have been levelled at this explanation of mugging. One is that, through its great stress on the wider situation, it almost completely ignores the people at the centre of the whole activity, the young muggers themselves. Their values and perceptions of the situation are ignored. To a large extent, this is a result of them being seen as innocent victims of a process of deviancy amplification (see pp. 62–63).

A second problem is that there is a contradiction in the study, in that on the one hand increasing police presence is necessary to maintain law and order which is supposedly under threat and, yet, the authors also claim that there was no actual increase in street crime. If there was no increase in crime rates why was there a threat to the power of the capitalists?

Corporate/white-collar crime

In *Power, Crime and Mystification* Box examines another concern of many Marxist writers—the extent to which crime is committed by large corporations.

Typically, crime is viewed as, for example, theft or robbery. Yet the significance of corporate crime goes unnoticed. According to Box, more people are harmed and more money is taken through the activities of large companies than all other forms of crime.

Firstly, he points out that activities which bring harm and financial loss to sections of the population are simply not regarded as criminal at all, when performed by industry and commerce. The use of harmful chemicals in food, of dangerous machinery in the workplace, the production of dangerous goods for profit, or even over-charging for products is not regarded as illegal.

This is partly a consequence of the *definition* of crime as robbery or theft and partly a result of the *power* of the large corporations to avoid the criminalisation of their activities.

Perhaps the clearest example of this is the exclusion of the financial institutions of the City of London from the law, in the sense that the City has the right to 'police itself'. Those engaged in dubious practices (by the standards of the City) are dealt with by the various 'commissions' of the city and only very rarely by the police. The police lack trained accountants and financial experts, as their role is seen to be the maintaining of public order and control of crime. This weak enforcement of the law is not confined to the City, however. In virtually all areas of industrial and commercial malpractice the enforcement agencies, (eg the Factories Inspectorate) stress not the consequences of the actions of the employers but the breaking of the particular regulation. For example, if a person shoots somebody else, he/she is unlikely to be charged only with illegal possession of a firearm! Yet, when it comes to injury as a result of defective machinery, at the most severe the company is likely to be charged with breaking the regulations concerning the machinery, and receive a small fine or letter of reprimand.

It has been pointed out that there is a crucial distinction between the actions of 'criminals' and those of industrial corporations, in that the criminals intend to harm people, while the harm caused by a chemical in an industrial process, for example, is unintended. However, Box contemptuously dismisses the argument that most harmful acts committed by corporations are unintended consequences of the legitimate pursuit of making a profit. He replies that most corporations are not concerned about the harmful effects on others. According to him there is a disdain for the rights of others which is just as serious as deliberately causing them harm.

As for the motivation of those who commit crime on behalf of the large corporations, Box suggest that they do so less from evil as from the need to conform with the demands of the organisation for which they work and the desire for promotion. Thus the fault falls less on the individual and more on the society which generates this sort of behaviour.

Here is an emerging new consensus on what crime *is*: the lawless acts of *unskilled* men. But if that is the meaning of crime, most fraud, bribery and corruption, many sexual offences, murder and a lot of domestic violence are written off as non-crime. *Does crime matter because of the money lost?* Fraud nets far more illegal gains than domestic and commercial burglary and goods-off-the-back-of-a-lorry put together. Estimates of current fraud losses a year range from the £1 billion counted in *The Incidence, Reporting and Prevention of Commercial Fraud* from the Police Foundation, to the £3 billion a year estimated by accountants Ernst & Whinney.

The British Insurance Association says that total theft losses from insured homes, commercial premises and goods in transit were £186.9 million for 1985. Even if this were doubled to take account of the quarter of households which are not insured and the burglaries which are not reported (though in both cases less valuable goods are likely to be involved) the amount stolen in commercial fraud towers above this. Does this mean middle class crime is destroying the fabric of capitalism?

Fraud like bribery and corruption and, at the other end of the scale, domestic violence, is somehow not regarded as *real* crime by many people. As was said when the Lockheed bribery scandal broke, it's just what businesses do. The provision of 'call girls' by large business or Foreign Office staff for their visitors is what is expected of them—not the indictable crime of procuring. Walloping their wives was seen for many years as what husbands did. Many private companies prefer to cover up evidence of fraud or bribery because it makes the company look bad.

Source: Benton, The Absence of Acceptable Authority, *The New Statesman,* 14 November, 1986

☐ 1 **What explanations do sociologists offer for the *definitions* of crime offered here?**

2 **There have been detailed studies of white-collar crime which are committed routinely. See, for example, Mars *Cheats at Work.*
Interview a person (who trusts you), and find out what activities are routinely performed which are illegal, or of dubious legality. Examples of this could be claiming excess overtime or 'fiddling' travelling expenses. An alternative activity would be to construct a list of offenses—perhaps using some of the examples given in the extract. Respondents should be asked to indicate how 'serious' the crimes are by giving each offence a mark from 1 to 5.**

3 **List some criminal acts which people regard as unimportant or at least acceptable.**

A pig rearing drug which was banned in Britain because it can cause cancer, must be put back on the market, the EEC has ruled. There will be no appeal and the Ministry of Agriculture admitted yesterday that it is powerless to prevent UK pig farmers from feeding the drug, known as carbadox, to their animals.

UK government scientists advised that carbadox should be banned in 1985 because it was a "genotoxic carcinogen." Feed-mill and farm workers were most at risk because they handled large quantities of the drug and even minute amounts of cancer-causing agents present health risks.

The drug was added to pig food to prevent swine dysentery but was also used as a growth booster to increase carcass weight and profits.

Pfizer, the US company which sold carbadox under the trade name Fortigro-S, withdrew the drug before the UK ban could be imposed but complained that the ruling was unjustified.

It took its case to the European Court of Justice in March after the EEC threatened a similar ban throughout the Community.

Dr Tim Lang, director of the London Food Commission, said: "It is outrageous that a drug company can use its muscle in the EEC to overturn the British ban, which was wisely imposed to protect both workers and consumers."

The only concession given to the UK is that warning labels will be printed on all feed bags, but Pfizer said yesterday that it believed that any hazard warning was unnecessary.

Source: Erlichman, 'Ban on pig drug lifted by EEC', article in *The Guardian*, 17 June, 1987

Drug companies Glaxo and Boots are to face a monopolies probe into the tight control they hold over the legal market for morphine and five other opium-based pain killers.

Suspiciously high profits made in supplying the drugs led Sir Gordon Borrie, the director general of the Office of Fair Trading, to announce a Monopolies and Mergers Commission investigation yesterday.

Glaxo and Boots are the only drug companies in the UK which have special licences from the Home Office under the Misuse of Drugs Act 1971 to manufacture the drugs. Glaxo's subsidiary, Macfarlan Smith Ltd, dominates the market and "appears to be making high profits," according to the OFT.

The Home Office licensing system also creates barriers to imports which, in a normal competitive market, would otherwise put a ceiling on domestic prices.

Source: Erlichman, 'A painful probe for two drug groups', article in *The Guardian*, 17 June, 1987

☐ **Look at the two articles above, taken from *The Guardian* on the same day.**
1 **Explain how they could be used to support a Marxist account of crime and deviance.**
2 **In what ways might critics of the Marxist approach be able to reject the Marxist explanation? Base your replies partly on the evidence in the two articles.**

☐ **PROJECT**

Examine newspapers, magazines, and television programmes in the past few weeks to find similar pieces of information which shed light on the Marxist approach.

Criticisms of the Marxist approach

The Marxist approach has been heavily criticised by both sympathisers and opponents.

One major problem has been the way it seems to ignore individual motivation. The stress is primarily on the nature of capitalism and the way that economic factors 'force' people to act in certain ways. Their perceptions, ideas and motivations are rarely discussed.

Second, Marxists seem to claim that the high rates of recorded crime amongst the working class, youth and blacks is solely the outcome of biased policing. At the same time they argue that the laws are biased against the working class, *forcing* them into crime. Critics point out that there appears to be a contradiction here.

Also, it seems rather dubious to explain all laws in terms of the interests of the ruling class—many laws could be argued to rest on genuine agreement. However, Marxists simply reject this form of

☐ **Using the themes of:**

1. **manipulation of values**
2. **law creation**
3. **law enforcement**
4. **individual motivation**

summarise the Marxist interpretation of corporate crime.

argument by claiming that even laws which *appear* to be for the benefit of society, are *in reality* of use ultimately to the ruling class. By providing a few laws that are of use to everybody, the real, repressive nature of the law is hidden. This infuriates critics, such as Mishra, who has called this form of Marxist analysis *left functionalism*, meaning that any law can be shown in some way to be 'functional' to the maintenance of capitalism. This makes any meaningful critical debate with Marxists impossible.

One final point which has often been raised is that societies which call themselves Marxist (whether they are not is a very different matter) appear to have at least as high a crime rate as the capitalist ones, yet in a Marxist society there ought not to be crime.

☐ **ESSAYS**

1 **Compare the Marxist view of law creation and enforcement with that of the labelling theorists. Illustrate your answer where relevant with examples.**
2 **What are meant by the terms 'white-collar crime' and 'corporate crime'? What importance do Marxists attach to this form of criminality?**
3 **What is the role of law in a capitalist society, according to the Marxist approach?**

Bibliography

S. Bowles and H. Gintis, *Schooling in Capitalist America*, RKP, 1976

Glasgow University Media Group, *Bad News*, RKP, 1976

P. Trowler, *Investigating the Media*, Unwin Hyman, 1988

S. Hall *et al*, *Policing the Crisis*, Macmillan, 1979

S. Box, *Power, Crime and Mystification*, Tavistock, 1983

R. Mishra, *Society and Social Policy*, Macmillan, 1981

R. Quinney, *Crime Control in Capitalist Society* in *Whose Law? What Order?*, W. Chambliss and M. Mankoff, Wiley, 1976

D. Gordon, *Class and the Economics of Crime* in *Whose Law? What Order?*, W. Chambliss and M. Mankoff, Wiley, 1976

Youth Unemployment—A New Social State, *New Society*, 29 March, 5 April, 12 April, 1984

The contemporary left has had considerable influence on sociology. It provides an approach which combines the *structural* perspective of traditional Marxism with many of the insights of labelling theory—in particular, the belief that any understanding of society must include an awareness of the *perceptions of individuals* and the importance of social reactions to perceived deviants.

The contemporary left in Britain developed from the work of Taylor, Walton and Young in *The New Criminology* and also from the Centre for Contemporary Cultural Studies at Birmingham University. Recently, there has been a split between those who stress the Marxist view in their work and *left realism*, most closely associated with Jock Young of Middlesex Polytechnic. The depth of these divisions is discussed in detail in Chapter 9.

The new criminology

The criticisms of the Marxist approach led to the development of *the new criminology*. In effect, this is a substantially modified version of Marxism. It places much greater emphasis on the perceptions of the 'criminals' themselves and on those who directly confront the 'criminals', for example the police, and analyses in detail the specific context in which crime takes place. The emphasis, therefore, moved away from studying how powerful groups create law for their own benefit, towards law enforcement, patterns of law-breaking and the motives of crime.

In *The New Criminology*, Taylor, Walton and Young suggest that sociological theories of crime ought to cover all of the following points:

The wider origins of the deviant act. This refers to the normal

Marxist point that all actions in society need to be understood in relation to the economic structure of society.

The immediate origins of the deviant act. This refers to the need to understand why individuals are motivated to commit crime. For example, it may be poverty or the desire for 'fun' that drives a person into the act of crime.

The act itself. Why should a person choose a particular act as opposed to any other? For example, why does one individual choose solvent abuse rather than football hooliganism?

The immediate origins of social reaction. Why do people respond in different ways to a particular deviant act? For example, do police officers respond differently to black offenders?

The wider origins of deviant reaction. This is the need to explain the wider background to law creation and enforcement. For example, studying the circumstances in which the decision to make certain forms of picketing illegal is made.

The outcome of the social reaction on deviants' further action. This refers to the need to understand how the 'labelled' criminals respond to their labelling. Clearly here the 'new criminologists' have been influenced by interactionist approaches.

The nature of the deviant process as a whole. This final point concerns the need to appreciate the sheer *complexity* of social action and not to force it all into simplistic models, such as in 'left functionalism'. If this makes the explanations exceedingly complex, then this is the price to be paid for fully understanding the nature of crime.

In the following sections we will first explore the contemporary 'subcultural' approaches to crime which have developed with, and alongside, the 'new criminology'. Secondly, there will be a detailed study of the attempts by Lea and Young (the founders of new criminology) to generate greater understanding of crime through the left-wing (though not necessarily Marxist) approach of *new realism.*

☐ **There is a chapter by Jock Young on deviance (in *The New 'Introducing Sociology'*, by Worsley et al), where he uses the 'new criminology' method to explain drug abuse. Take the model above and use it to analyse the explanation for drug usage. Does it work?**

Working class youth subcultures

The Marxist approach to crime and deviance spread far wider than an examination of the law. It also extended into an analysis of the more extreme, perhaps deviant, working class youth cultures. This presented a clear alternative to the traditional subcultural theories we examined on pages 30–40. Before examining the approach in detail, it is worth briefly discussing the functionalist view of youth culture, which provides a more conservative explanation for deviant behaviour amongst youth.

The functionalist approach

Traditionally, sociologists have regarded 'youth' as a period of *transition* from childhood to adulthood. The emphasis of the analysis provided by the *functionalist* school is that *all* youth has to find a way of moving from the secure, cosy world of the family into the competitive adult world of work, where individual talent and sharp competition with others bring the financial rewards.

The role of youth culture is to smooth the path from childhood into adulthood by providing a link between the conflicting values (or *pattern variables*) of the home (childhood) and work (adulthood). Eisenstadt, for example, has suggested that most young people seek to distinguish themselves from their parents, yet being different leaves them emotionally insecure. In response to this emotional insecurity young people create distinct sets of values and styles of dress. These serve the twin purposes of setting them apart from their parents (fulfilling the function of independence) and also providing them with a model or standard against which they can measure their behaviour. If I am a 'casual' for example, then I know how I ought to dress, the music I ought to listen to, and possibly the sort of behaviour expected of me.

Each generation of young people faces the same problem of transition and, therefore, creates a distinctive youth culture. Two points need noting here for comparison later with the Marxist approach. First, the actual *contents* of the youth culture (eg, the style of clothes adopted and the patterns of behaviour) are unimportant and need no further analysis. Second, differences in the backgrounds of young people and between the various youth subcultures are unimportant. The stress remains on the fact that all youth need some kind of *transition mechanism*, no matter what subcultural form it takes.

The Marxist approach

The Marxist approach to youth begins where the functionalists stopped. The Marxists stressed the importance of the *contents* of youth culture and the differences in *class backgrounds.* The Marxist approach is generally associated with Birmingham University's School of Contemporary Cultural Studies.

Hegemony

For all Marxists, capitalist society is characterised by *class conflict*, as a result of the ruling class's determination to retain control over the rest of society, and the resistance to this by the working class. According to the Marxist view, one of the major means by which the ruling class control people is to turn the cultural values of society to their benefit; for example, by claiming the *right* to have private medical treatment and the *right* to pass on wealth from one generation to another. This is done through control of the mass media and of values taught in schools. At this point, refer back to the notes you made for the activity on page 68. In Marxist terminology, the imposition of the ruling class's values on the rest of society is known as *hegemony.*

Youth

Most people in British society are so trapped by mortgages, credit repayments and general family commitments, that they are extremely nervous of any serious resistance to the status quo. The relative security of the contemporary capitalist system is seen to be better than the alternatives. In this way, the ruling class have successfully imposed their hegemony.

However, the least 'locked-in' group in British society is youth. Young people are relatively free of long-term financial commitments, have less allegiance to the family and are increasingly likely to be unemployed. They are, therefore, the weakest point in the structure of hegemony.

Resistance: the reason for youth culture

Functionalists argue that each generation faces the same problem of the transition from childhood to work. Marxists see the situation very differently. Each generation of *working class* youths face *similar problems*, of entry into routine, low paid employment, or no employment at all, but they do so in *different circumstances.* For example, the youths of the 1950s grew up in the aftermath of the Second World War, within very different cultural and economic circumstances from the youth of the 1980s. Writers such as Mike Brake in *The Sociology of Youth Culture and Youth* and Dick Hebdige in *Subculture: the meaning of style,* argue that the different generations of working class youth develop their youth culture as a means of coping with their problems, and the *styles* they develop reflect the particular cultural and economic circumstances of their generation. However, the activities of the youth culture indicate more than just 'coping', they also show a strong sense of *resistance* according to the Centre for Contemporary Cultural Studies. They actively show disdain for the dominant values of society, through their style of clothes and forms of behaviour.

Working class youth culture, which is often regarded as deviant and a threat to the wider society, is in fact an aspect of the class struggle.

Magic!

Earlier we saw how youth culture represents a way for working class youngsters to solve the very real problems they face. However, it is important to remember that the youths only solve their problems temporarily and only to their own satisfaction—the solutions provided by youth cultures do not really alter anything. For example, if you think you are unattractive and decide to combat this with lots of make-up, this does nothing to alter the structure of your face and body. The youth culture does nothing to alter the power and economic differences in society, which created the problems for working class youth in the first place. Mike Brake has, therefore, used the term 'magical' to describe the solutions provided by working class youth culture.

Resistance through style

A key element of the Marxist approach is that the *styles* the various youth cultures adopt are not meaningless, as the functionalist school would argue, but are deeply imbued with meaning. Through *style* working class youths work out their problems and express their resistance.

By 'style', sociologists mean the choice of clothes, haircut, haircolour, music, argot (slang) and 'ritual' forms of behaviour. Compare the cropped hair of the skinhead, for example, with the long hair of the 'heavy metal' fan. Much of the work of the Marxist subcultural school is concerned with decoding the hidden meaning of youth cultural style, in an attempt to see how the style denotes 'resistance'.

☐ **List any recent youth styles and then sub-divide them according to the elements given above. Now read the following section. Can you provide any sort of account for the development of the style? Work in small groups on the same style(s). Compare your answers. Is there any way to decide which is the correct answer? Does your conclusion to this last point provide a criticism of the approach in general?**

An example of the Marxist subcultural approach

One of the earliest studies using this form of analysis was that of Phil Cohen, who analysed youth in East London in the early 1970s. Cohen suggested that the only way to understand the meaning of youth cultures was to examine them in: a) their immediate context and, b) the wider context.

The immediate context. Cohen argued that during the 1960s the fabric of East London society had been ripped apart as a result of:

redevelopment—large numbers of people had moved out into new towns, or if they remained they were likely to live in high-rise apartments. Partly as a result of this, the close-knit street life was lost. Also the price of property rose as developers began to realise the potential of an area so close to the centre of London. The small workshops and businesses were driven out as rents and rates rose.

the loss of jobs on the docks—the economy of the traditional East End had been based on the docks, and the closeness of housing to employment had helped to create the feeling of belonging and community. After the decline of the docks in the 1960s, both the economic structure and one of the props of the community were destroyed.

decline of the extended family—partly as a result of the other two factors, the working class extended family also declined. This had consisted of a network of family members who provided each other with mutual support. Youth in the 1960s, therefore, had grown up without the traditional East End community to support them.

The wider context. The 1960s came as the benefits of greater affluence had percolated through to large sections of the population. Ownership of houses and consumer goods had risen sharply over the previous decade and a whole new ideology of affluence had begun to develop. This ran alongside the continuing existence of poverty and deprivation in inner city areas.

The resulting youth cultures. Youth cultures developed, according to Cohen, to cope with the loss of community, but they also reflected the divisions in society as a whole. Cohen suggests that two different responses occurred amongst youth. One element adjusted its sights and aspired to the new ideology of affluence—*the Mods.* The Mods wanted to show that they had money and knew how to spend it, on such things as mohair suits and Lambretta scooters. In contrast, the skinheads looked back to the more traditional working class community and through their clothes and actions adopted the short hair, the DMs, braces and tunic shirts of traditional working class men. By dressing this way, they were 'magically' saving the community of East London.

The following diagram illustrates how these contrasting types of behaviour produced a variety of youth subcultural styles.

Class and subculture: a version of Cohen's model

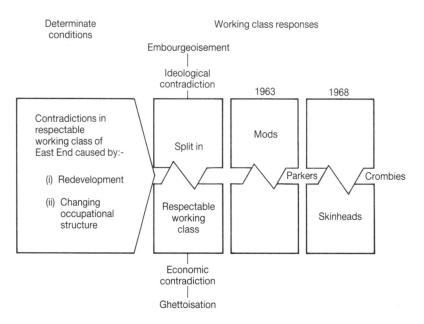

Study the diagram opposite. Do you think this sort of model can be continued into the 1980s?

Source: Hall and Jefferson, *Resistance through Rituals*, Hutchinson, 1977

Explanations for deviance: Marxist subcultural theory

First of all, it is important to remember that the vast bulk of crime (as conventionally defined) is committed by youth. Any theories that can explain the motivations of young people correctly will also provide the key to understanding crime.

By the 1960s, traditional subcultural theories (see pp. 30–40) were no longer appropriate, as they could not provide convincing explanations for the deviant activities of youth. The new Marxist-inspired approaches added important insights: they stressed that the activities, styles of dress and behaviour of youths all had *meaning*, which could be interpreted by sociologists. Secondly, that the activities of youth could not be understood without referring to the wider *structural* context of the economic and political system.

The impetus of the new subcultural approach led sociologists to examine a range of groups and activities.

Feminist writers argued that this approach ignored women. However, in defence of the Marxist subculturalists, it ought to be pointed out that the overwhelming bulk of criminal activity amongst youth is performed by males. The subcultural theorists were merely trying to find out why particular groups of males rebelled. However, feminist writers have since used the insights of the approach to examine the culture of adolescent girls (see pp. 41–42). Some writers, for example Ken Pryce, examined the situation of black youth in Britain (see pp. 124–125), while other sociologists took the issue of football hooliganism and examined this. Not all the writers accepted the perspective provided by the new Marxist subcultural approach, but it did provide the framework within which the debate took place.

Criticisms

☐ **The extract from *Folk Devils and Moral Panics* by Stanley Cohen attacks the way that Marxist subcultural theorists interpret the 'style' and activities of the deviant youths. Summarise Cohen's (rather difficult) criticisms under the headings**
1) bias in interpretation of a) style, b) actions,
2) the lack of interest in 'commercialism'
3) the romantic search for evidence of 'working class resistance'.

Before we examine the sociological contributions to our understanding of football hooliganism, we ought to bear in mind that the Marxist subcultural approach has been severely criticised.

First, as mentioned above, it ignored women and black people, concentrating exclusively on white working class youths. However, as we will see later there has now been considerable work done in this sphere, including the writing of McRobbie, and Griffin.

Secondly, Stanley Cohen has criticised this whole school of thought because its followers believe they have a special insight into 'decoding' the meaning of the styles adopted by the working class youth cultures. For example, in his study of racial attacks (Paki-bashing) in Lancashire, Pearson suggested that it was 'misdirected heroism', and drew a parallel with the Luddites. It could just as well be argued that the youths in question were simply racist (a traditional working class value) and attacked Asians for that reason. Why is one interpretation more correct than the other?

The Marxist subcultural approach has also been criticised because it implies that the sociologist always knows best. For example, the youths themselves may well give their own explanations for their behaviour, but the Marxist sociologists would discount these and argue that the real, *underlying* reason (of which the youths are unaware) is related to elements of the class struggle.

Both these themes of *resistance* and *symbols* are rich and suggestive. I have only the space to mention, somewhat cryptically, a few of the problems they raise.

The first arises from the constant impulse to decode the style in terms *only* of opposition and resistance. This means that instances are sometimes missed when the style is conservative or supportive: in other words, not reworked or reassembled but taken over intact from dominant commercial culture. Such instances are conceded, but then brushed aside because—as we all know—the style is a *bricolage* of inconsistencies and anyway things are not what they seem and so the apparently conservative meaning really hides just the opposite.

There is also a tendency in some of this work to see the historical development of a style as being wholly internal to the group—with commercialization and co-option as something which just happens afterwards. In the understandable zeal to depict the kids as creative agents rather than manipulated dummies, this often plays down the extent to which changes in youth culture are manufactured changes, dictated by consumer society. An allied problem is the often exaggerated status given to the internal circuit of English working class history. The spell cast on the young by American cultural imperialism is sometimes downgraded.

This is inevitable if the subculture is taken to denote some form of cumulative historical resistance. Where we are really being directed is towards the 'profound line of historical continuity' between today's delinquents and their 'equivalents' in the past.

These theorists subscribe to what Ditton nicely calls the dinosaur theory of history. A recent zoological argument apparently proposes that dinosaurs did not after all die out: one group still lives on, known as— birds! Similarly, historical evidence is cited to prove that mass proletarian resistance to the imposition of bourgeois control did not after all die out. It lives on in certain forms of delinquency which—though more symbolic and individualistic than their progenitors— must still be read as rudimentary forms of political action, as versions of the same working class struggle which has occured since the defeat of Chartism. What is going on in the streets and terraces is not only not what it appears to be, but moreover is really the same as what went on before. And to justify this claim, a double leap of imagination is required. In Pearson's example, the 'proof' that something like Paki-bashing is a 'primitive form of political and economic struggle' lies not in the kids' understanding of what it is they are resisting (they would probably only say something like, 'When you get some long stick in your 'and and you are bashing some Paki's face in, you don't think about it') but in the fact that the machine smashers of 1826 would *also* not have been aware of the real political significance of their action.

This seems to me a very peculiar sort of proof indeed.

Source: Cohen, *Folk Devils and Moral Panics,* 2nd Ed., Martin Robertson, 1980

Football hooliganism

The initial explanations for football hooliganism came from within the broad approach of the Marxist subcultural school, and has branched out more widely since then.

Territoriality

Most of the subcultural explanations for football hooliganism have centred around the idea of *territoriality.* Working class youths have a sense of owning and controlling their local environment. Throughout the studies of gangs from Chicago, New York, Glasgow and Liverpool, a recurrent theme is territorial control and the showing of contempt for other gangs by ritually invading their territory.

This theme has been picked up by sociologists seeking an explanation for crowd violence at football matches. Clarke argues, for example, that the tight, white, working class communities which the football clubs originally represented in inner city areas, no longer exist. Redevelopment, economic change, and changes in the ethnic 'mix' have broken up the community. The clubs too have altered. Local footballers have been replaced by well-paid professionals brought in from outside and the grounds are often owned by outside interests. So, both the local community and the clubs have become 'lost' to the contemporary generation.

According to Clarke, the activities of the football hooligans are a form of recapturing and recreating the lost community. The 'end' symbolically represents the community (or 'territory') and defence of this 'magically' (see p. 80) solves the problem. Attacks on other fans' 'territory' serve to strengthen allegiance and the sense of belonging of the youths engaged in violence. This approach has been strongly supported by Robins and Cohen in their study of North London youth (*Knuckle Sandwich*).

Ian Taylor has also suggested that this loss of community, allied to the split in the working class between the more- and less-affluent, led white working class youths into racial violence as a form of *displacement* of their frustration.

The symbolic nature of violence

The work of Marsh, Rosser and Harris (*The Rules of Disorder*), is not within the Marxist subcultural school, but provides a detailed account of actual behaviour of the fans in more detail. Their study consisted of a detailed ethnographic account of 'fans' of Millwall and Oxford United football clubs.

On closer examination the apparently disorganised behaviour of the troublemakers was found to be fairly structured. At the Oxford United ground, the fans at the 'end' were divided into groups based on age and patterns of behaviour.

Marsh *et al* discovered the following divisions:

Novices	10–11 year olds
Rowdies	15 upwards, who were subdivided into: hooligans, hardcases, nutters
Town boys	19–25 year olds

The novices were too young to join fully in the activity on the terrace and they provided an admiring audience for the Rowdies. At the other end of the age range were the Town Boys who were tough men who had been through the stage of being Rowdies and already proved themselves. The final and core group of the 'end' were the Rowdies, who could be subdivided into three:

the *hooligans*: their behaviour was primarily aimed at fooling about and making fun of the opposition fans.

the *hardcases*: these were the toughest group and would be the ones most closely involved in violence.

the *nutters*: these were the ones who were unpredictable and most likely to engage in extreme violence. These were regarded by all other groups as 'out of order' on occasions.

Marsh *et al* claim that most of the 'aggro' was, in fact, *symbolic* and *ritualised*, and that relatively little violence occurred. All participants, with the exception of the 'nutters', accepted that there were limits which it was wrong to go beyond. The belief in the extent of violence was created partly by the boasting of the youths themselves after the matches and partly by the activities of the media who exaggerated the extent of violence.

Furthermore, Marsh *et al* claim that much of the resentment of working class youths concerning their position in society was expressed through their Saturday afternoon confrontations. It was a form of *catharsis*, in which their pent-up feelings were dissipated. See pages 35–36 for a comparison with Cohen's work.

The multi-causal approach

Williams, Dunning and Murphy in *Hooligans Abroad*, are critical of the previous two approaches. They argue that the claim of Marsh *et al* that little violence takes place is incorrect; their study indicates quite considerable levels of violence. They also criticise the simplistic approach put forward by the Marxist subcultural theorists, Williams *et al* argue that the idea that football violence is a manifestation of the current crisis of the working class community is inaccurate in so far as there have been serious levels of football violence throughout this century—even during the times when the Marxist subcultural theorists state there was a cohesive, functioning working class community. If this is the case, then football violence cannot be the result of the collapse of the working class, inner city community.

The model they propose is one which takes into account the fact that the values which give place to football violence have always existed in working class culture. However, the extent to which these values are expressed in football violence, or some other arena depends upon specific factors which change over time. They argue that football violence has come to the fore as a means of expressing certain working class values, because of a combination of the following factors:

the structural changes that have occurred within and between upper and lower sections of the working class; the rise of the specifically teenage leisure market; the increased ability and desire of young fans to travel to away matches on a regular basis;

□ **PROJECT**

It may not be possible for you to check on all these theories, but you could select a particular area of interest. Is there really violence or is it merely symbolic? Are there distinguishable groups at the 'end'? Devise a means of studying your chosen area and then visit local football grounds.

the changing racial contours of British society; specific attempts by the football authorities and the government to curb football hooliganism; changes in the mass media, particularly the advent of television and the rise of the modern tabloid press; and last but by no means least, the recent virtual collapse of the youth labour market.

Source: Williams, 'Football Hooliganism' in *The Social Science Teacher*, Vol. 15 No.3

The new criminology of left realism

In this chapter, we have examined the varieties of *Marxist structural* theories. There still remains one version which is of profound importance in today's sociology. The significance of this approach is that it manages to combine in a clear and sensible way many of the better ideas of traditional criminology.

First, this approach *contrasts* with other *Marxist* approaches, *positivist* approaches, and *conservative* approaches to crime.

Second, the key elements of this approach centre on the concepts of *subculture, marginalisation* and *relative deprivation.*

The reality of crime

Traditional Marxist approaches to crime have generally rejected the view that the high official crime rates of the working class are an outcome of harsher policing (police harrassment) and the deliberate imposition of laws which benefit the rich at the expense of the majority of the working class. The left realist viewpoint starts from the position that the official crime rates really *do* reflect high rates of crime by the working class. This debate emerges most forcibly in the argument between Gilroy and Young (discussed on pp. 118–120). This may not seem too radical an argument, but to the 'left' in Britain, accustomed to making the working class and blacks the heroes, and the police the villains, it is quite a major step. The confirmation of the official crime statistics emerged from two major studies of crime on Merseyside and Islington, London. These showed high rates of crime committed by working class male youths, primarily on working class people, in the most deprived areas. Indeed, one of the most important new findings of the Merseyside and Islington surveys was the genuine fear and concern about crime felt by most inner-city people.

The new left realist approach takes the view that, although white-collar crime rates are significantly higher than the official statistics would suggest, the sort of crime that worries people most, particularly in the inner cities, is primarily performed by young working class youth, white and black.

Once the official statistics of crime were accepted, there was less emphasis on the study of law creation and enforcement (the central elements of the traditional Marxist model) and there was then a need to look again at the *causes* of crime.

There is little new in the left realist position, it consists more of a synthesis of a number of ideas which have been around for some considerable time. These ideas focus on three elements: *subculture, relative deprivation* and *marginalisation.*

Subculture

The model of society proposed by the theories of left realism consists of a multiplicity of groups which have developed their own variations of value, within the mainstream culture, as a response to their own problems. It is true to say, therefore, that the police have their own subculture (as they face particular problems) just as much as working class black youths have subcultures of their own.

The subcultural model proposed by Lea and Young has a number of distinguishing features, including:

Subculture as a response to problems. Those who are most likely to commit street crime have developed their own cultures as a response to their particular problems and position in society. They are not necessarily aware of this, nor is it necessarily true to say that the subculture provides them with a true solution—nevertheless the subculture is a means of solving their problems. (See the discussion on the Marxist subcultural approach to youth culture, pp. 79–80.)

The macro–micro dimension. The 'problems' which people face are not randomly distributed. They are the precise results of a political and economic system. Capitalism ensures that some people are far worse off than others and considerably less powerful (This is quite clearly a structural model. See p. 72.)

The objective/subjective balance. The views of the members of the subculture are important but not necessarily the 'reality' of the situation. On the other hand, it is not right for sociologists and other observers to read into the actions of the members of the subculture the meanings they would like to exist there. (This is a reference to the criticisms of the Marxist youth culture approach made by Stanley Cohen. (See p. 83.) So a balance has to be made between the views of sociologists and those involved in the subculture, though one needs to ask just how Lea and Young propose to do this.

The subculture is not completely separated from the values of the wider society. The distinctive values of subcultures are not divorced from the wider society, rather they are closely enmeshed in those values. They are distinct not separate. This is important, because Lea and Young argue that it is precisely *because* of the acceptance of British society's material goals that young blacks, for example, feel relatively deprived. (See the discussion on Matza and subterranean values p. 37 and race and crime p. 127.)

The historical dimension. The subculture is not passed on from one generation to the next, but is recreated by each generation according to their experiences and the context in which they live. These contexts change over time. (See, for example, the debate on race and crime pp. 125.) So, the working class do not have an alternative set of values as Miller suggested (see p. 36), but they do have constantly changing sets of values reflecting the broader changes in society.

☐ **Look up the references suggested in this chapter in the discussion of subculture. Write a paragraph on each. Are they useful in understanding the approach of Lea and Young?**

Relative deprivation

One of the most interesting pieces of Young's argument is that unemployment and poverty are not directly the causes of crime. The unemployment/crime link has become a cherished notion of most liberal and socialist politicians in recent years and the rejection of the link has caused a considerable stir amongst the Left.

Young explains his argument by pointing to the old notion of relative deprivation. People measure their situation against social expectations provided by society. A person may well be poor in some objective sense, but may not feel poor if all those around him or her are in the same financial situation. On the other hand, by making a different comparison, the same person could feel poor and aggrieved. The feeling of being deprived is relative to one's expectation.

Young points out that in the 1930s, the levels of unemployment were roughly the same as in the mid–1980s, yet the level of crime was fifteen times higher. Poverty can not be the cause for this, as one of the poorest groups in society is the elderly, yet they commit the lowest number of crimes of all groups.

According to Lea and Young, contemporary youth feel frustrated and bitter because of the disparity between their high expectations and the reality of what they can actually obtain, given the levels of unemployment and the low-wage jobs on offer.

As we saw earlier, the values of subculture are not sharply distinct from the general set of values in society. Working class youth accept the dominant values of society and accept those aims too—but their behaviour is modified by the circumstances in which they find themselves; to put it simply, at the bottom of the heap. Therefore, they develop strategies to enable them to solve their problems, and this can involve crime.

An alternative approach to crime and unemployment

Unemployment *does* lead to increased criminal behaviour, according to a new report providing what are probably the hardest data so far collected on the much-debated relationship between crime and joblessness ('Unemployment, school leaving and crime,' Farrington *et al*, in the *British Journal of Criminology*, Vol 26, No 4).

Theoretical and common-sense hypotheses that increases in unemployment will lead to rising crime have previously been dogged by the difficulty of establishing causal links between aggregate crime and unemployment rates. Other intervening factors, such as the validity of unemployment statistics and changes in the exercise of police discretion in dealing with offenders, have also made interpretation extremely difficult.

But this new study by Farrington and his Cambridge colleagues has circumvented most of these difficulties. Using a group of 411 mostly working class males studied since they were eight or nine years old, the researchers analysed data from the period before and after leaving school when the youths were 14, 16 and 18 years old. They were therefore able to compare the youths' educational and job histories with their

officially recorded criminal behaviour over time. This demonstrates quite conclusively that unemployment does lead to greater offending, though the nature of the relationship is not straightforward.

First, taking all youths whatever their job history, there were roughly three times as many offences committed during periods of unemployment as when the youths were employed. Since this straightforward comparison might mask the fact that employed and unemployed youths differ in some other respect which affects the likelihood of them committing offences, Farrington also looked at the 193 youths with mixed periods in and out of work. This showed offending rates twice as high during periods of unemployment (0.51 compared to 0.23 offences per year).

Not all types of offending were increased by unemployment, and neither were all unemployed youths prone to react criminally. Unemployment led to a significantly increased number of offences for material gain (theft, burglary, fraud and so on), but other offences (such as assault, criminal damage and drug offences) were unaffected.

It was also clear that higher levels of offending during unemployment occurred only with those youths who were already at greatest risk—those with low income parents, from large households, in poor housing, with relatively neglectful parents, and of low educational achievement.

Farrington is careful to remind his readers that these data were collected in 1968–72 when unemployment was relatively low. The group studied were also almost entirely white. Nevertheless, the message is stark, particularly for the inner cities. Those young men (for crime is predominantly the activity of young men) who are relatively advantaged are likely to be able to ride a period of unemployment. But those who are already disadvantaged are likely to turn to crime as a result of the additional blow of joblessness.

After this evidence, politicians will find it far harder to justify the oft-repeated claim that unemployment does not cause crime.

Source: Morgan, 'Jobless turn to crime, study shows', article in *New Society*, 14 November, 1986

☐ **1 How does this approach differ from the left realist approach?**
2 This is an excellent example of the 'positivist' approach discussed on pages 40–41. Explain *why* this is a good example.
3 What methods would sociologists use to uncover any possible links between crime and unemployment?

Crime and unemployment

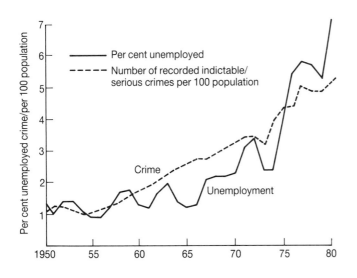

The figure reproduced from Tarling (1982) above, details the trend of crime and unemployment during the period 1950–80. He comments on this relationship as follows: 'The association between the two over the entire 30 year period was very strong. But within this period the evidence was not uniform; the association during the first half—1950 to 1965—was much weaker and not statistically significant. Because crime has generally been increasing, any other series that exhibits the same overall trend will be highly correlated with it. It would not be difficult to find a range of other measures, some obviously irrelevant, which mirror the crime figures equally as well and more consistently throughout the period. Indeed, the consumption of alcohol, the consumption of ice cream, the number of cars on the road and the Gross National Product are all highly correlated with rising crime over 1950–1980.' (Tarling, 1982)

As if that were not enough, the problem of the ecological fallacy presents itself. This fallacy would in this context be the argument that because unemployment and crime go up together, crime is being committed by the unemployed. To recognize this as a fallacy, one has only to take the hypothetical case of an increased use of public transport and a decreased incidence of road deaths. This should not lead us to the conclusion that it is the people who took to the buses who would have killed people while driving their cars! Likewise it should not be concluded that it is the unemployed who are to blame for the extra crime. Stevens and Willis (1979) analysed white, black and Asian arrest rates and various demographic factors, including rates of unemployment for the same three ethnic groups. Their results were too complex to report in full, but it is fair to take their analysis of assault as an example. Arrests of whites for assault co-varied with white unemployment rate but not with Asian or black unemployment rates. However, Asian arrest rates for this offence did not co-vary with any of the unemployment rates and black arrest rates co-varied with rates of unemployment for all three ethnic groups! There was thus no neat correspondence between arrest and unemployment rates within a particular ethnic group.

Source: Bottomley and Pease, *Crime and Punishment—Interpreting the Data* pp 138–9, Open University Press, 1986

☐ **Taking the information from the main text and the two extracts on cime and unemployment, construct a diagram/chart to summarise the various positions.**

'What's so special about this left realist stuff, they've just fiddled around a bit with Merton's anomie and stuck it on to a Marxist perspective like the ones used by the Marxist subculturalists. Oh yes, and there's a bit of Matza'.

☐ **(Quote from a class discussion on left realism.) Do you think there is any truth in this? Read pp 76–104 of Lea and Young's, *What is to be Done about Law and Order* (See Bibliography for this chapter).**

Marginalisation

The third element of the left realist approach concerns the concept of *marginalisation.* This means the process by which certain groups find themselves 'on the edge' of society, in both an economic and political sense. White and black working class youth, especially in inner city areas, face particularly great problems in terms of their high rates of unemployment. However, Young points out that there is a political dimension beyond this.

A number of pressure groups and political organisations have developed over the years to force the voice of the working class to be heard and some of their demands met. The strength of the working class lay in its economic muscle, for example the strike, and to some extent in the feeling of community in the working class districts of the towns. However, youth has no such economic muscle, or political or community organisation. They are marginal to both the economic and political systems.

Before the extension of the franchise towards the end of the last century, there were legal channels through which the working class could influence political decisions. The only outlet available to them was through political demonstrations or through riots. For Lea and Young this represents the situation of 'marginalisation' that the young, and particularly black youth, find themselves in today.

Criticisms of the left realist position

This approach is currently 'fashionable' in sociology. However, it has been subject to three basic criticisms. First, more orthodox Marxists criticise its stress on working class crime and its causes. They suggest instead that much more attention needs to be paid to white-collar crime and to the process of law creation. Lea and Young have replied that they agree corporate crime is 'worse', but that in everyday life it is street crime that worries people.

Second, many more orthodox sociologists outside the Marxist tradition wonder why it is such a magnificent 'breakthrough' to realise that the official statistics on crime are roughly correct and that all along the young, the working class and blacks in inner cities have disproportionately higher rates of crime than other groups in society.

Third, what is so new about the approach anyway, it is claimed? In many ways it follows the guidelines of traditional subculture, and Mertons's anomie, and placed these ideas within a more radical Marxist perspective.

Crime: a comparison of the traditional Marxist and left realist approaches

Traditional Marxist approach

This approach is associated with Chambliss, Qinney, etc.

Criminal statistics. Incorrect, biased in that they ignore the extent of middle class crime, corporate crime, etc. The statistics reveal much more of a bias in the activities of the police and in the law-making process.

Who commits crime? All sections of society. However, the real criminals are within the ruling class.

Structural perspective. Relates criminal acts to the wider structure of society.

Values. Manipulated by the ruling class via media, education etc.

Police. Repressive. Reflect the interests of capital.

Community attitude to police. Negative, feel repressed and search for means to fight back against them.

Focus of research. Law creation, police activity.

Causes of crime. Repressive, biased laws. Class struggle, unemployment, poverty.

Race. Black crime rate higher because of biased policing. Black crimes a response to oppression and part of a tradition.

Female crime. No comments. Accepted that women have low rates of crime, primarily because they are excluded from productive process.

What policy should be adopted towards crime? Crime is seen as a form of rebellion against capitalism and, therefore, is a good thing on the whole. Criminals are admired, as expressing a neo-political act.

The left realist approach

This is associated with Jock Young.

Official crime statistics. Generally correct, reflecting the concerns of the majority of people, including the working class. Accepts however, that corporate crime/middle class crime is greater than the official statistics state.

Who commits the crime? All sections of society, but mainly the young male working class.

Structural perspective. The criminal acts have to be viewed within a wider structural perspective.

Values. The values of society are partially manipulated as the orthodox Marxists suggest. However, people also genuinely create their own subcultures in response to their problems.

Policing. Repressive, but reflects the will of the majority of people.

Attitudes of the community to the police. Positive overall. Trouble occurs when there is a breakdown in communications between police and community.

Causes of crime. The outcome of subculture, marginalisation and relative deprivation.

Race. Extreme marginalisation. Those of West Indian origin likely to have higher crime rates compared to Asians because they have higher levels of relative deprivation and marginalisation.

Female crime. No coherent position. However, accepted that women do have lower rates of crime.

Policy towards crime. Crime most affects the working class and they need the greatest assistance from a sympathetic police force. Need to work towards the recreation of working class communities and better police/public communication.

☐ **ESSAYS**

1 How have Marxist approaches helped us to understand youth and delinquency?
2 Football hooliganism has attracted considerable attention in the media recently. What explanations have sociologists offered for this phenomenon?
3 In recent years left realism has developed to challenge the dominance of orthodox Marxist ideas. What is left realism? What distinguishes it from other approaches?

Bibliography

I. Taylor, P. Walton and J. Young, *The New Criminology*, RKP, 1973

J. Young, *Working Class Criminology* in I. Taylor *et al, Critical Criminology*, RKP, 1975

P. Worsley *et al, The New Introducing Sociology*, Penguin, 1987

S. Eisenstadt, *From Generation to Generation*, The Free Press, 1956

P. Cohen, *Subcultural Conflict and Working Class Community,* in *Working Papers in Cultural Studies* No. 2, The University of Birmingham, 1972

M. Brake, *The Sociology of Youth Culture and Youth Subculture*, RKP, 1980

D. Hebdidge, *Subculture, the Meaning of Style*, Methuen, 1979

K. Pryce, *Endless Pressure*, Penguin, 1979

A. McRobbie *Working Class Girls and the Culture of Femininity* in Centre for Contemporary Cultural Studies (eds) *Women Take Issue*, Hutchinson, 1978

C. Griffin, *Typical Girls? Young Women from School to the Job Market*, RKP, 1985

S. Cohen, *Folk Devils and Moral Panics*, Martin Robertson, 1980

S. Pearson, *'Paki-bashing' in a North Lancashire Cotton Town: a case study and its history* in *British Working Class Youth Culture*, ed G. Mungham and G. Pearson, RKP, 1975

J. Clarke, *Skinheads and the Magical Recovery of Community,* in *Resistance Through Rituals*, ed. S. Hall and T. Jefferson, Hutchinson, 1976

D. Robins and P. Cohen, *Knuckle Sandwich*, Penguin 1978

P. Marsh, E. Rosser and C. Harris, *The Rules of Disorder*, RKP, 1980

Williams, Dunning and Murphy, *Hooligans Abroad*, RKP, 1984

T. Jones *et al, The Islington Crime Survey*, Gower, 1986

R. Kinsey, *The Merseyside Crime Survey*, Merseyside Metropolitan Council

J. Lea and J. Young, *What is to be done about Law and Order?* Penguin, 1984

7 · Crime and Gender

'Oh, *that's* why men commit more crime than women !'

Source: adapted from an advertisement in *Marxism Today*

This chapter explores the nature of female criminality, an area largely ignored by sociologists to date. For this reason, female crime has been described as the *invisible* area in sociology. The first task, therefore, is to explain just why it has been ignored. We then need to examine the extent of female crime as revealed in the official statistics, and to see whether they reflect the true extent of female criminality.

Finally, we will explore the explanations offered for female crime (or the lack of it!).

Invisible women

Virtually every sociological theory of crime manages to exclude any serious discussion of women. Examine any of the key sociological texts from the main theoretical perspectives of Marxism (Chambliss, Hall), functionalism (Durkheim and Merton), subculture (Chicago, Cohen, Downes) and labelling (Becker). What they all have in common is the dismissal of women to footnotes, except for discussions on prostitution. Traditional (and contemporary) sociology of deviance is a 'sociology of the boys'. How did this occur? Frances Heidensohn in *Women and Crime* has suggested that there are four reasons for this:

vicarious identification,
male domination of sociology,
lower recorded levels of female crime,
the nature of the theories of the sociology of deviance.

Vicarious identification. Male sociologists were attracted to the sort of life and subcultural activities which delinquents exhibited. It was thrilling to 'bring back news from the fringes of society, the lower depths, the mean streets'. Yet, these sorts of investigations were not traditionally possible for female sociologists. The 'mean streets' were 'off limits' to them. Also, the male sociologists who did study the lives of working class adolescents were generally precluded by their interests and their sex from studying the lives of working class girls.

Male domination of sociology. Although the overwhelming number of students of sociology are female, the teaching of the subject—particularly at the Higher Education level—has been dominated by males. Male assumptions have therefore become entwined in the roots of the subject.

Lower recorded levels of female crime. A number of male sociologists have tried to study female crime but were unable to uncover anything. For example, in his classic study of 1,313 gangs in New York, Thrasher could find only one delinquent female 'gang'. We shall examine the statistics of female crime on page 94.

☐ **Take a cross-section of the theoretical approaches to crime you have studied (eg, Merton's anomie theory, or Cohen's subcultural theory). Examine the extent to which they can be used to explain female criminality.**

Theories of deviance. Heidensohn argues that the theories of deviance proposed by the male sociologists simply accepted stereotyped ideas on females. She suggests that all the theories of crime already developed could be undermined by asking how they could incorporate an explanation for the rates of female crime? For example, if Cohen was right and young working class adolescents become frustrated leading to delinquent behaviour, then what about the girls? Wasn't Merton's model of anomie implicitly based on potential male responses? The Marxist theories were too concerned to analyse elements of *social class* that they overlooked (by and large) the divisions of gender in society. Before feminism developed, there were no available theoretical tools to develop models which could incorporate explanations of the female crime.

The statistics of female crime

Persons found guilty or cautioned for indictable offences

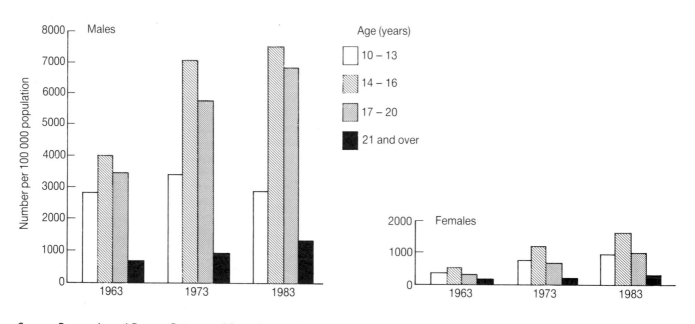

Source: Bottomly and Pease, *Crime and Punishment: Interpreting the Data*, Open University Press, 1986

The official statistics of crime are quite clear, that overall males are five times more likely to commit crimes than females. By the age of twenty-eight, when the levels of offences falls to an extremely low level, 33 per cent of males and 6 per cent of females have been convicted of a 'serious' offence. However, it is important to note that, in the last twenty years, the increase in female crime has been threefold, while for males it has been twofold. It's most notable that crime is an activity for the very young female. The peak age for offences is 13–15 for girls, (whereas for males it is 14–18). However, the age spread for females committing crime has been widening rapidly, so that there has been a doubling of rate for 10–12 year olds and tripling for 14–17 year olds. Apart from different

levels of crime and slight differences in the *ages* of criminals, there are also some significant differences in the *types* of offences. Below are a few examples of the differences—the numbers represent the male:female ratio:

Serious motoring offences 30:1
Burglary 25:1
Robbery 20:1
Violence against the person 10:1
Theft and handling 3:1

The only crime in which females exceed males is shoplifting.

Official criminal statistics

A number of writers have suggested that the criminal statistics do not reflect the extent of female crime.

Masked female crime

The first person to claim this was Pollack, writing in the 1950s, who argued that much of female crime was *masked* and gave the examples of prostitution and shoplifting which are commonly not reported to the police.

The true crime level

To find out the true crime level sociologists developed the techniques of *self-report studies.* Basically, these involved asking samples of girls to read through a list of deviant acts and to tick those they had committed at some time. This technique was used by Campbell for example, and she concluded that instead of a 7:1 male/female crime ratio, there was one of about 1.2:1, indicating that the levels of crime were more or less equal for males and females.

However, there appears to be some doubt over the validity of Campbell's research. When questions concerning trivial offences were excluded from the self-report studies for females, the official female crime ratios were much nearer the official ratio for male crimes.

Steven Box reviewed all the available evidence and concluded that overall the proportion of female to male offences may be underestimated by the official statistics, but that when it came to *serious* offences, it is quite clear that the official statistics are a fairly accurate guide.

Differential treatment by the police and courts

A bitter debate has developed in sociology concerning the treatment of women by the police and courts. American studies by researchers such as Kalven and Zaesel suggest that there is a 'chivalry factor' which encourages juries and judges to be more lenient towards women. In Britain, NACRO (National Association for the Care and Resettlement of Offenders) has commented that a number of special factors influence magistrates and judges in their approach to the sentencing of women. In particular, factors such as the exclusive responsibility for running the home and caring for dependents, or the fact that an offender may be pregnant, are typical examples (See NACRO, *Women in the Penal System*, 1980). The result is that twice as many women are cautioned, (rather than being prosecuted) and a higher proportion receive a discharge.

An extreme alternative position holds that courts are actually harsher with female defendants. They claim this is because the 'juvenile court functions as a management tool, equipped to correct . . . female behaviour which . . . flaunts normative expectations by challenging family authority and threatening truancy and sexual promiscuity,' (Casburn, *Girls will be Girls* quoted in Heidensohn, *Women and Crime*).

When the magistrates' magazine *Justice Of The Peace* questioned a group of judges about the criteria they used in passing custodial sentences, one reply read: 'In the case of some children or girls, behaviour which was unchildlike or unfeminine.' It's difficult to imagine a boy standing accused of "unmanly behaviour," yet we lock up our naughty daughters for behaviour which would gain scarcely-veiled approval when committed by a son.

"Boys will be boys," and boys are naughty. A son's overnight absence will probably earn him no more than a knowing wink from dad, just as his drunk and disorderly behaviour is "all part of his growing-up." Even a minor offence is not the end of the world: at least he's got *balls.* But while a little-girl-tomboy is all very cute, parents, especially fathers, find it difficult to accept disobedience in a teenage daughter, whom they see as refusing to conform to the behaviour expected of her sex. For failing to come home on time, hanging around in the wrong part of town, or adopting dubious friends, a girl is far more likely than a boy to be declared "in moral danger" for which, at the instigation of her parents, school, social worker, or the police, she may be taken into the care of the local authority.

Persistent rebellion—not unlikely in the circumstances—will prompt her transfer into "secure accommodation" where the girl who "needed protection" makes friends with fellow delinquents and more serious juvenile offenders, and is statistically more likely to become an offender.

These same discriminatory attitudes which insist that a girl must be locked up for behaviour which would be unremarkable in a boy, bear down with full force on the girl who strays into the world of petty crime.

Girls' most popular crimes are theft—usually shoplifting—criminal damage and assault. (Unlike boys, however, who generally assault strangers, girls tend to assault people they know.)

The criminal justice system sees girls as offending not only against society but against their true natures as well. Unruly boys have their high spirits beaten out of them at detention centres but—tough and controversial though the method may be—unless their crimes are particularly violent or perverse, there is not the suggestion that there is anything fundamentally wrong with the boys.

Criminal girls, on the other hand, are maladjusted: *real* women would not commit crime because *real* women would not jeopardise their domestic role—of caring wife and mother—and its rewards.

Social enquiry reports, which may be requested on juveniles by the court, dwell on a boy's choice of friends and social habits, whereas a girl's parents are more likely to be questioned about their daughter's willingness to help with housework and the washing. Girls who have previously been declared beyond control or in moral danger, and older teenagers who are homeless, single mothers, drug or drink dependent, or who have a child in care, are far more likely to be locked up than those living more conventional lives.

Because it is assumed that girls receive more police cautionings before they are first prosecuted, by the time she appears in court a girl is assumed to be more delinquent than her male peers and is more likely than them to receive a custodial sentence, rather than a fine or community service order, for her *first* conviction and therefore at an earlier age.

Source: Ingram, 'Trials and Errors', *The Guardian*, 17 February, 1987

In fact, the truth of the matter seems to be more complicated than the two polarised positions would have us believe. Courts do seem to operate on a double standard when it comes to female criminals. Light sentences seem to be imposed on those who fulfil the traditional role of the female, while women who do not fit normal gender patterns, or whose behaviour offended traditional 'moral codes' are more likely to receive harsh punishment.

A similar debate has taken place over the attitudes of *police officers* towards female offenders. Are they likely to treat them more leniently? We do know that far higher numbers of females are simply cautioned compared to males—45 per cent of boys and 70 per cent of girls were let off with cautions in the early 1980s according to Mott's study. This may be because police officers hold stereotyped beliefs concerning young females—for example, they are more likely to be led astray by male companions or that boys are more likely to be criminal types than females etc.

☐ **It has been found that female police officers have higher arrest rates of women. Could you suggest any reasons for this, based on** the information in the last paragraph and your knowledge of gender roles? Possibly the following quote from the **Policy Studies Institute** study (in 1984) of the Metropolitan police may help: 'Ideas about sex, drinking and violence are linked together in a cult of masculinity which is thought to provide the key to the criminal world.'

Biological explanations for female crime

Early explanations for female crime were generally based on some presumed biological differences between males and females. At the turn of the century, the Italian criminologist Lombroso studied female criminals and found that they were abnormal because they lacked some of the 'natural' female traits which included *reserve, docility* and *sexual apathy.* He found that the female criminals were very like men in that they had 'exaggerated sexuality'—ie normal sexual desire.

Lombroso's writing can be dismissed as a historic relic, but in the same way that male deviance is still explained by some 'experts' in biological terms, so there are recent explanations for female deviance using this framework.

In 1968, a study by the researchers Cowie, Cowie and Slater found that, in general, girls have a higher level of immunity than boys to 'environmental stress' (meaning such things as an unhappy home life), and it is only when 'constitutional predisposing factors' exist that they will turn to crime. In essence, therefore, crime is: 'related to biological ... differences, including differences in hormonal balance; and these would at the ultimate remove be derived from chromosomal differences between the sexes.'

In the 1980s came the first mention of *pre-menstrual tension* in criminal cases, based on the theory that the stress caused by menstruation could cause women to act irrationally and in such instances they could not be held responsible for their actions.

Criticisms of biological explanations

Biological explanations have been criticised on a number of grounds. The greatest criticism against them is that they confuse gender roles with biological sexual differences. It is not that women are biologically docile and sexually passive—they are brought up to be that way through the processes of socialisation.

Also, biologically-based theories ignore the fact that laws are *social constructions.* Laws are created by people and vary from society to society and over time.

Psychological explanations for female crime

Biological and psychological explanations have become closely entwined in criminology. Eysenck's psychological theory of the cause of crime is equally applicable to both males and females. Eysenck argues that there are two basic personality types—extroverts and introverts. He believes that extroverts are the ones most likely to commit crime.

Eysenck tested his thesis on groups of married and unmarried mothers. According to Eysenck, being an unmarried mother is a sign that the person is more likely to be promiscuous and, therefore, deviant

1. **The last extract referred to 'unfeminine' and 'unmanly' behaviour in the first paragraph. What do these terms generally mean to most people? (You would certainly need to do some research to answer this question— possibly a questionnaire or interviews).**

2. **It has been suggested that female crime is related to the ways that males and females are socialised into gender roles. Could you suggest any explanation along these lines?**

3. **'Girls' most popular crimes are theft— usually shoplifting ...' Can you offer any explanation for this? It might be a useful exercise if you interview local shop managers about this (especially in fashionable clothes shops).**

4. **'Because it is assumed that girls receive more police cautionings ...' Why is this assumed? How could you find out if it is true or not? DO it!**

(see p.134 of *Crime and Personality*). According to this research, the unmarried mothers were found to be both more extroverted and also to have much higher degrees of emotionality and neuroticism than did the married mothers.

Talcott Parsons has also suggested a theory which links the disciplines of psychology and sociology. Parsons claims that in American society, the male adult role model is work-centred, while the woman's is home-centred. He suggests that male delinquency is a result of childhood identification with the mother. After the childhood or 'latency' years are over—during which time males and females are 'home-centred'—culture demands that the male adopt a masculine or 'job-centred' role. In response to this, youths react strongly against all traits associated with femininity, and this initially excessive 'masculinity' can sometimes lead them into delinquency. For the majority of girls the move towards an adult female role model is not problematic and so does not lead to delinquency. Female crime can, therefore, be related to either the influence of the dominant male in adulthood or the result of some problem in socialisation in the latency period (perhaps being brought up by the father).

Contemporary sociological explanations for female crime

Traditionally, the few studies available of female crime have concentrated on finding the differences between 'normal' women and deviant women. Because it was assumed that women were *naturally* less likely to commit crime than men, the most common explanation was to stress the way that criminal women showed 'manly' characteristics.

Recent feminist approaches to female criminality have been directed less at explaining what special attributes female criminals have and more at examining *why* so few females commit crime compared to males. It is suggested that the answer to this can be found in three areas:

> different socialisation and stricter social control,
> fewer opportunities for women to commit crime,
> an unwillingness to take the risks of breaking the law.

Reasons why the female crime rate is lower than the male

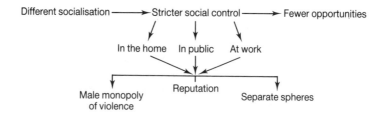

Different socialisation

It is a standard sociological argument that the expectations of behaviour associated with each of the sexes—gender roles—are created through the process of socialisation.

From infancy children are taught that the two sexes are different and that there are clusters of attributes which males and females ought to have. Female roles contain such elements as attractiveness, softness, caring, sweetness and domesticity. Male roles, on the other hand stress elements such as toughness, aggressiveness, sexuality.

☐ **Gender differences include: The games they play/the language used to describe them/their forms of dress/the toys bought for them/the books and magazines published/the subjects considered suitable for study at school and after/the types of employment they should aspire to. Give examples for each of the differences in socialisation above.**
Refer to textbooks on the sociology of gender.

As a result of socialisation, girls could be said to be 'lacking' in the values which are generally associated with delinquency, particularly the elements of toughness and aggressiveness associated with masculinity in our society.

This approach is supported to some extent by the low levels of conviction of females for violent street crime. This is the area where there is the largest difference in the numbers of convictions of men and women. The offences for which females are more likely to be arrested than males are shoplifting and prostitution, and these can be tied in with the different sex role expectations for females. For example, shoplifting derives from the role of mother and family-provider and prostitution from the other element of the female role, that of sexual provider in exchange for economic benefits.

Social control

Socialisation and social control are concepts that cannot be clearly distinguished: they overlap and mutually strengthen one another. While reading this section, remember that the controls men place upon women's behaviour also become embedded in the consciousness of women.

It is the area of social control which has attracted most attention from feminists recently. Their point is that women are less likely to commit crime not from any natural streak of goodness and kindness but rather from the fact they spend most of their lives being controlled by men into law-abiding roles. Females are therefore far more constrained than males in their lives.

Women and the home

Some feminists compare the nuclear family to a prison in which women are trapped. Women are constrained in their nuclear families through ideological bonds, based on the belief that they ought to be the ones who look after children and that this should be done to the highest standards possible. Women who 'fail' in the role of mother and housewife are the butt of family and community disapproval, as the culture of British society stresses that the primary role for a woman is as wife and mother. The same constraints do not apply to males, so that husbands are merely expected to 'help' their wives in the home.

The effect of these ideological expectations of society on women is to lock them into a narrow, family centred role, controlled to a large extent by men.

Heidensohn suggests in *Women and Crime* that where women fail in the demands imposed upon them control may take the physical form of violence against them (see pp. 110–114 on marital violence).

There are relatively few acceptable ways for women to escape the pressure of control in the family and one of these, according to Procek, is through neurosis or depression, rather than crime.

☐ **'Women's mental illness is the form taken by their power struggle within the personal space of the family' (Procek *Psychiatry and the Social control of Women*, 1981). Looking at page 54, what are the gender differences for mental illness? What other factors can be suggested to explain the different levels of mental illness?**

One important point is however, that women go *willingly* into marriage and the domestic role associated with it, as a result of their earlier socialisation into gender roles.

The social control of women in public

The way that male expectations of female behaviour in the home constrains the freedom of women is continued in the wider public treatment of women. Three examples of the constraints on women in public are:

>   the male monopoly of violence,
>   fear of a 'bad' reputation,
>   the dominance of 'public' life by men.

The male monopoly of violence. Culturally and historically, men have maintained a monopoly over the use of violence. Females are simply not socialised, as some men are, into the use of violence as an acceptable means of resolving problems. The Rambo figure is adored by both males and females alike, the army consists primarily of men, and war is a 'man's game'.

Fear of a bad reputation. Females are expected to be far more passive than men in sexual matters and girls who are 'forward' are likely to suffer through a 'bad reputation'. This will attract male interest in trying to have sex with them, but will also scare males off from seeking long term relationships. In an interesting study of how girls are labelled by boys into categories such as 'slag', or 'tight bitch', (*Losing Out*), Lees has shown how this labelling can have major consequences on the way girls behave. No respectable boy would like to be seen going out regularly with a 'slag', for example. Conversely, the girls hated being labelled as a 'tight bitch'. The result was a cautious (and narrow) line between the two extremes. According to Lees, there are no equivalent expressions to describe boys. Nor is the behaviour of males as closely controlled in sexual matters as that of females.

The domination of the public world by men. Men and women inhabit different worlds. For women, the sphere is the *private* one of home and the public areas connected with it, such as the supermarket. The male sphere is the *public* one. The workplace, the streets at night, pubs—

these are more male preserves than female ones. In pubs, for example, single women are made to feel uncomfortable and the general view (by males) is that they must be there to 'look for a man'. Indeed the majority of places outside the home pose a threat to women. Quite simply, you usually have to go out to commit crime, and women do not go out!

☐ **PROJECT**

Devise a number of different ways of examining how women are controlled by men (eg, observing male responses to women in pubs or checking on Lee's argument by asking males how they categorise females etc). How do women see this control? Does it influence their daily lives?

Opportunity to commit crime

The result of socialisation and control is that women have less desire and less opportunity to engage in deviant, risk taking or criminal acts. During adolescence, for example (the peak of crime for both sexes), they are far more likely to be confined to the home as the result of the parental social control mentioned earlier. Girls have therefore, according to McRobbie and Garber, developed a *bedroom culture*, consisting of girls visiting each other to play records, practise dance moves and chat. This is different to the male adolescent culture in that it takes place indoors, not out on the streets, where opportunities for delinquent behaviour might arise.

In adulthood, females are constrained through the material demands of looking after their husbands and children, through housework and cooking for example, which takes all their time and energy. Free time for other activities is severely limited. Interestingly, the only serious crime in which women are represented in greater numbers than men is shoplifting; being out shopping represents one of the few areas where women actually have the opportunity to commit crime.

In employment, women are generally restricted to lower level, routine employment and therefore rarely have the opportunity to engage in white-collar crime.

When it comes to crimes involving violence, again women are at a disadvantage. The socially accepted female role does not include toughness or aggressiveness, and women who express these 'masculine' traits are not rewarded. It is therefore likely that they will not be drawn to this form of crime.

Finally, women are unlikely to be in the position to have the knowledge to commit crime. The sort of technical knowledge required to steal a car, or even a car radio, may be more readily available to the male reading motoring magazines (generally aimed at a male audience), whose casual conversation may well be about the 'masculine topic' of the relative merits of different motor cars.

☐ **The explanation which I have given for differences in the rates of crime is rather complicated. It consists of three key areas: different socialisation/stricter social control/and fewer opportunities to commit crime. Each of these has then been further subdivided. Make brief notes on each division and subdivision, using the diagram on page 98 as your guide. Please** note that I have included the social control of women at work in the diagram, but I will leave it to you to find out how women are repressed and controlled in the work situation.

Conclusion

The feminist argument is that women are both socially and psychologically restricted by men in their lives. The outcome is a much greater propensity to conform to strict rules, which curb females from a wide range of behaviour, part of which is deviance.

☐ **ESSAYS**

1 **The most noticeable thing about women in criminological research is their absence! What explanations can you suggest for the 'invisibility' of women?**
2 **What explanations have sociologists offered for the lower levels of convictions of women for criminal offences?**

Bibliography

F. Heidensohn, *Women and Crime*, Macmillan, 1985

O. Pollack, *The Criminality of Women*, University of Pennsylvania Press, 1950

A. Campbell, *Girl Delinquents*, Blackwell, 1981

S. Box, *Power, Crime and Mystification*, Tavistock, 1981

National Association for the Care and Resettlement of Offenders, (NACRO), *Women in the Penal System*, 1980

J. Cowie, B. Cowie and E. Slater, *Delinquency in Girls*, Heinemann, 1968

H. Eysenck, *Crime and Personality*, Paladin, 1970

S. Lees, *Losing Out*, Hutchinson, 1986

A. McRobbie and J. Garber, *Girls and Subculture* in *Resistance through Rituals* eds S. Hall, T. Jefferson, Hutchinson, 1976

J. Hargreaves, *Sport, Culture and Ideology*, Routledge, 1982

The true extent

The statistics

We have seen that women are less likely than men to *commit* crimes. But, are they also less likely to be the *victims* of crime?

The results of the *British Crime Survey* show that women are far more concerned about crime. For example, 35 per cent of women aged 30–60 felt 'very unsafe' in British streets after dark, compared to only 4 per cent of men. Yet, according to the same source, women are actually slightly *less likely* to be attacked than men, so that 1.6 per cent of men in that age group are victims, compared to 1.4 per cent of women.

Sexual harassment?— you get used to it

I don't let it bother me.....

☐ **PROJECT**

Fears of personal safety after dark and risks of 'street crime', according to the *British Crime Survey*:

	% likely to be victims of street crime	% feeling very unsafe
Men		
16–30	7.7	1
31–60	1.6	4
61+	0.6	7
Women		
16–30	2.8	16
31–60	1.4	35
61+	1.2	37

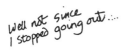

Well not since I stopped going out.....

Construct a simple questionnaire about the level of fear about 'street crime' in your college or locality. You will need to: (a) break down the types of street crime into mugging, sexual assault, etc. and; (b) categorise your replies by factors such as sex and age. Include in this some interiews with women about how they feel the fear of crime affects their behaviour (see below).
What conclusions can you draw from your study?

The myth of women as victims

Some sociologists, such as Clemente and Kleinman (*Fear of Crime in the United States*, 1977) argue the fears of women are exaggerated and that the chances of sexual assault, for example, are minimal for the average woman. They point to the fact that there are only 16 sexual assaults for every 100,000 members of the population. Compare this, for example, to the proportion of 410 burglaries for every 100,000 people or 1,490 acts of vandalism.

From this has developed the theory that the media exaggerate the extent of sexual crimes. They do this because of the unfortunate fact that reports of crimes such as horrific rape cases are newsworthy events that sell newspapers. Women themselves receive a distorted image of the dangers of going out after dark and as a result fear going out and stay indoors. As so many women avoid walking in the streets at night or travelling by public transport, the streets become emptier and the fewer people in the streets at night, the greater the chance of an assault going unseen, The result is that the minority of women who choose to go out at night are in greater danger.

The following diagram illustrates this process, as outlined by Clemente and Kleinman:

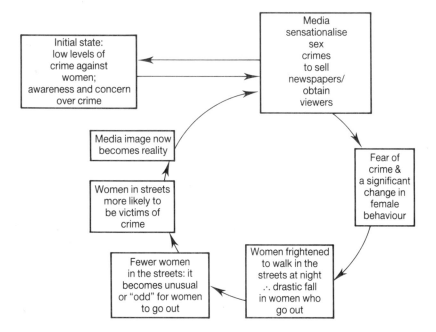

In effect, this argument dismisses the fears of women as unreal. As Clemente and Kleinman argue, 'Fear of crime ... has become a problem as serious as crime itself'.

The differential exposure approach

This approach argues that certain groups of women really are more likely to be victims of crime than men. The argument has two parts:

(a) that female victims are highly *concentrated* amongst certain groups and in certain areas of cities. Overall, rates may be low but in inner cities they are very high indeed. Women's fears are, therefore, justified in these areas.

(b) that the types of crimes specific to women, that is, sexual assault and marital violence are those *least likely* to be reported and recorded in official statistics.

Studies like the Home Office's well-known *British Crime Survey* have revolutionised thinking about crime. By asking people direct about the crimes they have experienced, such studies give us a much more reliable measure of the extent of crime.

However, national studies do not trace the way in which crime is finely concentrated, for example, in the inner city. These are often lost in global figures for the country as a whole.

With this in mind, the London borough of Islington

last year commissioned the Centre for Criminology at Middlesex Polytechnic to conduct a survey of the extent of crime in the area, and to assess the public's evaluation of police performance. A random sample of 2,000 households were surveyed.

Foremost, our study showed the substantial impact of crime on the lives of people in the borough. A full third of all households had been touched by *serious* crime (for example, burgulary, serious robbery or sexual assault) in the last twelve months.

Crime shaped people's lives to a remarkable degree. A quarter of all people *always* avoided going out after dark, specifically because of fear of crime, and 28 per cent felt unsafe in their own homes. There is a virtual curfew on a substantial section of the female population. Over half of the women never or seldom went out after dark, because of their fear of crime.

It is sometimes suggested that crime, although frequent, is a minor irritant, given the range of problems the city dweller has to contend with. The public, on this view, suffer from hysteria about crime. Panics abound—particularly about mugging, sexual assault and violence—which are out of touch with reality. These arguments are backed up by evidence from sources like the *British Crime Survey*, which says that the "average" person can expect "a robbery once every five centuries ... a burglary every 40 years ... and a very low rate for rape and other sexual offences."

But the inner city dweller is not the average citizen. Our study, with its ability to focus in on the highly victimised, indicates the realism of their fears.

It is scarcely odd that 46 per cent of people in Islington should admit to worrying "a lot" about mugging, given that over 40 per cent of the borough's population actually know someone (including themselves and their family), who has been mugged in the last twelve months. Nor is it unrealistic to worry about burglary when its incidence in the borough runs at five times the national average.

Why are women more fearful about crime than men, when most studies show they have a far less chance of becoming victims? Our survey suggests that, in the inner city at least, their fears are perfectly rational. Women here are more likely to be victims of crime than men.

The reason for the shortfall in past findings is the nature of many of the crimes committed against women, and their reluctance to admit them to a stranger engaged in a social survey. Using carefully trained, sympathetic researchers, we found a considerably higher rate for female victims. The reason is threefold: sexual assaults are almost exclusively a female "prerogative"; so is domestic violence; and street robbery against women is greater than it is against men.

In terms of non-sexual assault alone, women in the borough are 40 per cent more likely to be attacked than men. Sexual assault in Islington is 14 times the national average. A fifth of the women we interviewed knew someone sexually assaulted or molested in the previous twelve months. Over half had experienced sexual harassment of a non-criminal kind.

And all of this occurred even though the women took much greater precautions against crime than men. They were, for example, five times more likely never to go out after dark than men; three times more likely to always avoid certain types of people or streets; and, very significantly, six times more likely, to always go out with someone else, instead of alone.

Source: Jones and Young, 'Crime, police and people' article in *New Society*, 24 January, 1986

☐ **The *British Crime Survey* is a national survey in which people were asked which crimes they had been the victims of.**
  1. **What significant differences occurred in the findings between the BCS and the Islington survey?**
  2 **Why were the findings so different between the two surveys?**
  3 **What does this tell us about the national statistics of crimes against women?**
  4 **Brownmiller, a feminist writer, has suggested that the fear of sexual assault which women have ... 'is nothing more or less than a conscious process of intimidation by which all men keep all women in a state of fear'. In your opinion does the fear of assault limit the freedom of most women? Devise an appropriate method of conducting a small survey to answer this. Do you accept that it *is* a 'conscious process of intimidation' by men?**

In the United States, where most of the research has been done, the relative rates of rape vary significantly amongst different groups. For example, a poor black woman is six times more likely to be raped than a rich white woman, and a woman aged 16–19 is seven times more likely to be raped than one aged 35–49.

In Britain, the *Merseyside Crime Survey* showed that in some parts of the inner city, *half* of all women under the age of fifty said that they had been 'upset' by some form of sexual harassment in the streets.

However, it is not just sexual harassment that occurs primarily against women. The *British Crime Survey* suggests that the overwhelming number of victims of bag-snatching and mugging are women. Again, this form of crime is specific to inner city areas.

These points lead Lea and Young (see *What is to be done about law and order?*) to suggest that certain categories of women living in inner city areas really are more likely to be the victims of criminal attacks, and it is not an irrational fear.

A further criticism of the 'myth of females as victims' approach, concerns the fact that the crimes most commonly committed against women—rape and marital violence—are the ones least likely to enter the official statistics, as we shall see in the following two sections.

Rape

Rape statistics—reports and reality

In Britain in 1987 about 2000 rapes were officially recorded as being reported to the police. However, the *British Crime Survey* found that 28 per cent of sexual assaults were reported to the police, and a similar Scottish survey found that there were only 7 per cent reported. Even these figures appear to be an underestimate, however. The *British Crime Survey* states: 'The survey showed a very low rate for rape and other sexual offences ... leaving aside definitions problems and any sampling error, some under-counting of such offences committed by non-strangers may have arisen from respondents' reluctance to relive a painful or embarrassing experience for the benefit of a survey interviewer'.

The relationship of rapist to victim

The most commonly-held view of rape is that it occurs in a dark alley, late at night and is committed by a stranger. The reality is rather different. In a breakdown of rapes reported to the *London Rape Crisis Centre*, 54 per cent of the victims had been raped by somebody they already knew—bear in mind, too, that there appears to be a strong reluctance in a woman raped by a friend or relative to tell anybody at all, so even this figure is likely to under-represent the proportion raped by someone they know. A second point is that children are highly unlikely to have contacted the Rape Crisis Centre and these are the most likely to have been raped by a close relative.

Relationship of assailant to woman

Sample: 281

Relationship	Number	Percentage
Stranger	128	46
Acquaintance	82	29
Position of trust	24	9
Known—friend	24	9
—lover/husband	13	4
—relative	10	3

Source: Sexual violence: The Reality for Women, The Women's Press, 1984

Where rapes occur

The second point is that only about one-third of rapes take place in the street or in some isolated spot, the same percentage that take place in the home of the victims.

Explanations for rape

Traditional explanations

The traditional explanation offered for rape focuses on:

the natural sexual drive of the rapist,
the precipitating actions of the victim.

The diagram below outlines this:

Different explanations for rape

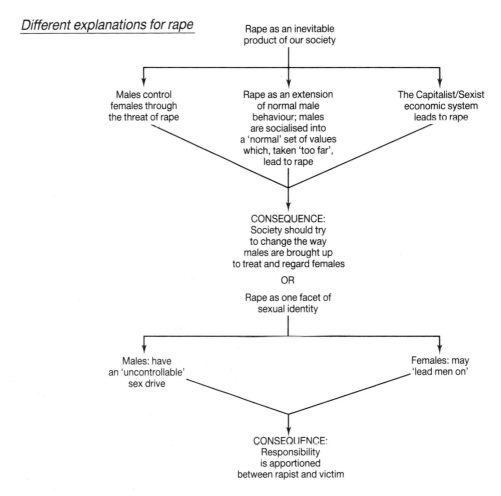

The rapist. Commonly he is regarded as a man who is unable to control his overwhelming sexual desires. Usually, he is incompetent or frustrated in sex and as a result may turn to rape. Interestingly, this explanation is often linked to a defence of prostitution, which is seen as allowing a sexual outlet for men who would otherwise suffer from complete sexual frustration. This is, in essence a *biologically-based* explanation as men are viewed as having powerful sexual drives which must be fulfilled. It also implies that women do not have the same degree of sexual desire.

The victim. The second element of the traditional approach to rape centres on the victim. Women are sometimes seen as encouraging the rape through their manner or style of dress. The psychologist, Horney, has even suggested that some women are masochistic and may actually enjoy rape. This may cause them subconsciously to 'lead certain men on' whom they find attractive.

Another version of *victim theory* concerns the fact that although women may actually enjoy sex, they are culturally expected to limit their sexual contacts, so the 'advantage' of rape is that it allows them to perform sexual intercourse, but frees them of the associated guilt.

The *consequences* of these traditional beliefs concerning rape are quite profound. For the victims themselves, if the person who rapes them is known to them and is to all extent and purposes 'normal', then was it really rape? And were they partly to blame for some remark, style of dress or attitude? This may lead some women to decide not to report the rape to the police.

The police and judiciary. Most men (and, therefore, police and judges) perceive rapists as significantly different from 'normal' men. Those who rape are a distinctive category, suffering from certain biological, psychological or social problems. Therefore, when confronting a person accused of rape, his apparent normality and the fact that he is often known to the victim contradicts the stereotype of the typical rapist and leads them to distrust the accusation of rape. They may also harbour suspicions concerning the actions of the victim which they may interpret as having led up to the rape.

The radical feminist perspective: rape as control

A completely different interpretation of rape comes from the feminist perspective. Brownmiller, for example, has argued:

> ... from prehistoric times to the present ... rape has played a critical function. It is nothing more or less than a conscious process of intimidation by which all men keep all women in a state of fear ... men who commit rape have served in effect as frontline masculine shock troops, terrorist guerrillas in the longest sustained battle the world has ever known. (S. Brownmiller, Against Our Will, *Secker and Warburg, 1975*).

Brownmiller argues that rape is a '*conscious*' act by men to retain control over women, and although it is performed by relatively few men, it clearly serves the purposes of *all* males.

The feminist perspective: rape as 'normal' behaviour

In *Women, Crime and Criminology*, Carol Smart argues that rape is to some extent 'normal' in a society in which the women are *expected* to engage in sexual bargaining. According to her view, the very basis of marriage has traditionally been the exchange of regular sexual favours by women for the security of the relationship. Smart points out that the images of women portrayed in the media and the attitudes socialised into both sexes from an early age stress the importance of sexuality and attractiveness of females.

Furthermore, men are encouraged to seek sex, and women to put up an initial resistance before 'giving in'. Indeed, a woman who appears to encourage sex is regarded as 'loose' by many men. The men are, therefore, *encouraged* to be active (possibly even aggressive) and the woman to appear reluctant.

The significance of Smart's argument is that rape is not some distinctive, deviant act which is *opposed* to the normal sexual relations in our society, rather it is an *extension* of normal sexual values and gender relations.

The Marxist–feminist perspective

This approach has most clearly been proposed by Steven Box in *Power, Crime and Mystification* who has suggested that rape is a result of:

> *... the historical conjuncture of 'sexist male culture', coupled with gross inter- and intra-gender inequalities in wealth, power and privileges, and firmed up by techniques of neutralisation and a legal system in which institutionalised sexism is embedded, that forms the roots of rape.*

☐ **Devise a method for finding out the attributes people regard as 'manly', then list these. Can this be related to the argument for the different reasons for rape?**

This is rather a densely-worded explanation, so it may be useful to break it up into smaller parts:

Sexist male culture. He argues that in British culture women are regarded as inferior and their social worth is measured by their attractiveness. We examined this earlier, when we looked at Smart's argument.

Gross inter-gender inequalities. Men hold most significant positions of power. For example, in employment males are more likely to hold the managerial and supervisory positions. Therefore, Box argues, various forms of sexual harassment may be tolerated at the workplace by women, in order to keep in the bosses' good books.

Techniques of neutralisation. Matza originally suggested the idea of techniques of neutralisation in his explanation for juvenile crime (p. 37). Briefly, Matza suggested that there are cultural 'excuses' which we all use to justify ourselves when we commit deviant acts—for example 'I didn't know what I was doing, I was drunk'. Delinquents merely carry these excuses a bit further to justify their behaviour. Box suggests that there are culturally-acceptable excuses for rape too and these include the idea that women put themselves in situations where they are more likely to be raped (eg hitch-hiking), so they are partly to blame.

Institutionalised sexism in the legal system. The assumptions which the police and the judicial courts act upon when dealing with rape reflect, according to Box, the sexist attitudes of the wider society. The idea discussed above that rapists must be in some way 'abnormal', for example, means that judges (possibly juries) and police officers find it hard to believe that ordinary men like themselves could possibly be guilty of rape. The fault must therefore lie somewhere with the victim. We can see that sociological analyses of rape have therefore moved away from placing the stress on biological urges, or psychologically-disturbed individuals, towards the situation where rape is seen as a normal outcome of our society. The approach is Marxist because it locates these elements within the framework of capitalism.

☐ **Examine the contents of daily tabloid newspapers. Do they support the feminist perspective on sexuality?**

Marital violence

The extent of marital violence

In *Violence Against Wives*, a study of violent offences in Edinburgh and Glasgow in the mid–1970s, the Dobashes found 25 per cent of all offences recorded by the police consisted of assaults by men on their wives. Yet, this figure is a massive underestimate of the extent of such assaults. The Dobashes' research suggests only 2 per cent of assaults on wives are ever reported and in *Sociological Perspectives on Family Violence* Marsden has calculated that serious violence takes place in about 5 per cent of all British families.

The reporting and recording of marital violence

There are two groups of people who play a crucial role in influencing the statistics of marital violence: the assaulted wives, and the police.

Wives. Wives are reluctant to report assaults against them for the following reasons. First, fear that the reporting of violence to the police or social services will only lead to further violence against them.

Second, many wives regard the violence against them as a personal matter between themselves and their husbands and may be too embarrassed to report it.

This ties in with the third reason, that a wife may sometimes blame herself for her husband's violence. She feels she may in some way have 'deserved' the violence as a result of her inadequacy as a wife.

Finally, some wives believe that the police are largely indifferent to their plight.

The police. Police officers view some degree of conflict between spouses as quite common and not necessarily to be regarded as 'serious'. The level at which a 'simple' marital dispute becomes an assault is left to police officers' discretion. The Dobashes argue that police officers will interpret these in a loose manner, basically operating on the belief that a little violence to keep a bad wife in her place is not a bad thing, although 'excessive' violence is unjustifiable.

A second factor influencing the police decision to prosecute derives from a belief that wives are likely to *withdraw their complaint* after a short 'cooling off' period. Interestingly, of those cases which do proceed, only about one in ten women withdraw their complaint.

A third and crucial factor influencing the perceptions of police officers is that of privacy. In *Marital Violence and Public Policy*, Pahl has stressed the importance to police officers (and the law in general), of the distinction between acts committed in a 'public place' and those committed in a private home or institution. In British culture, the right of a person to the privacy of his/her own home is strongly emphasised; anything which takes place within its confines is regarded as the personal business of the family.

The above three factors all conspire together to make the police extremely reluctant to intervene in domestic violence.

Types of physical force used during violent episodes

Physical force	Typical Violent episode N	% of total
Slap or push/pull into non-injurious object	78	15
Punch face and/or body	226	45
Push/pull into injurious object	19	4
Kick, knee, or butt	140	28
Attempt to drown, smother, or strangle	9	2
Hit with object/weapon	26	5
Other (bite, stand on, rape)	8	1
Total	506	100%

Note: Up to five different types of physical force in any single violent episode were recorded. These figures reflect only the different types of physical force used and not the number of times each type was used.

Types of injuries resulting from the worst violent episodes

Injuries	Worst Violent episode N	% of total
Bruises to face and/or body	182	64
Abrasions	2	1
Burns	4	1
Cuts	48	17
Hair torn out	13	5
Fractured bones or broken teeth	11	4
Internal injuries, miscarriages	8	3
Knocked unconscious	14	5
Total	282	100%

Note: 'N' is the total number of people interviewed. Up to five different types of physical injuries in any single violent episode were recorded. These figures reflect only the different types of injuries, and not the number of times a particular type of injury was received.

Third parties contacted by women after violent episodes

Third party	First N	First %	Worst N	Worst %	Last N	Last %
Parent, other relative	37	33	47	19	42	11
Friend	20	18	20	8	33	9
Neighbour	13	11	24	10	23	6
Doctor	21	13	53	22	43	12
Minister	3	3	5	2	3	1
Social worker	6	5	35	14	63	17
Police	12	11	35	14	47	13
Women's aid	—	—	14	6	93	25
Other	1	1	13	5	24	6
Total contacts	113	100%	245	100%	371	100%
Number of women making contacts	52		88		105	

□ **Study the above three tables.**
1. **Who are women most likely to contact?**
2. **Why do you think they do not go to the police?**
3. **What does this tell you, if anything, concerning women's attitudes to (a) marital violence, and, (b) the police?**
4. **How would you describe the sort of marital violence used against women?**

Source: All three above tables are from Dobash and Dobash, *Violence Against Wives*, Open Books, 1979

Explanations of marital violence

Explanations for marital violence fall into three general categories. The first of these stresses the *individual* and looks for defects in his personality or background. Broadly speaking, this falls in with the *positivistic* approach to the explanation of crime. Here, the argument is that as 'normal' men do not assault their wives, then violent husbands are abnormal in some way. This approach then looks for the differences between the normal husbands and the violent ones.

The second approach stresses the distinct *subcultural values* held by men who assault their wives.

The third approach stresses the *structural* context in which the violence takes place. The behaviour of the violent husband is not seen as solely a result of his defects, but also as a result of a society which allows, or even promotes, violence against wives.

The individual

In the mid−1970s, Faulk (in *Men who assault their wives*) studied men who had been convicted of assaulting their wives. He concluded that the majority of them could be classified as *mentally ill.* So, wife assault represented the actions of a few disturbed individuals.

It should be noted though, that the sample was not at all typical, as it consisted of men who had been *convicted* of violence against their wives. If the extent of under-reporting of marital violence is as great as suggested earlier, then these men could hardly be regarded as typical.

Alcohol has also commonly been associated with marital violence. Pahl, for example, found that 52 per cent of husbands in her sample 'often drank to excess' according to their wives, and this has been supported by a majority of other studies. However, the Dobashes study of violence in Scotland found only 1 per cent of attacks were precipitated by heavy drinking. The question of why the men drink heavily in the first place also needs to be considered.

Violence in the childhood home was blamed by Strauss, Gilles and Steinberg in *Behind Closed Doors: Violence in the American Family,* as the cause of adult violence. People who grew up in violent homes were more likely to use violence than those who had not. One in ten husbands who grew up in violent families used serious violence against their wives. Of course, the obvious criticism of this explanation is that nine out of ten husbands who used violence against their wives grew up in households where violence was *not* normal!

Other *psychologically-based* approaches have followed the line of investigation into childhood experiences and Schultz, for example, argued that wife assaulters are likely to have had 'domineering, rejecting mother relationships'.

Finally, one last group of researchers have stressed the *deviant nature of the husband−wife relationship*, suggesting, for example, that where a wife is 'aggressive' and tries to 'control the relationship', the husband may turn to violence. We seem here to be returning to an approach which 'blames the victim', as we examined earlier in our discussion on the causes of rape.

The subculture of violence

☐ **Looking at the reasons given for the under-reporting of marital violence (see p. 110), suggest reasons why there may be differences in reporting levels between working class and middle class women.**

If you were to conduct a study of marital violence what methods would you use?

The second explanation for marital violence moves the spotlight away from the individual specifically, and instead focuses on the subcultural values of the violent individual. Wolfgang and Ferracuti, for example, examine the way in which certain working class groups are brought up to regard violence as acceptable behaviour. This helps to explain why the bulk of reported marital violence occurs amongst the working class.

There are some major problems with this approach, however. They centre around the fact that we cannot be sure marital violence really does occur mainly among the working class. Middle class women may be less likely to report it. According to the 1975 Government Select Committee on marital violence:

> *Most witnesses agreed, and this is almost certainly correct, that all strata of society are involved although the better off are perhaps less likely to seek outside help.*

If we accept the argument that marital violence is spread throughout society, then the claim that there is a specific subculture of violence, restricted to the working class, must be wrong. For, if the behaviour is widespread, then so must be the belief in using violence against wives. Therefore, marital violence does not derive from a subculture but is part of the general culture of contemporary British society.

Structural explanations

This final type of explanation, generally associated with the *feminist position*, is based on the argument that marital violence is not isolated, deviant behaviour which runs against the generally accepted values. Instead, it is argued that marital violence happens due to the low status of women in society (and in the family in particular) and the belief that the male ought to be the dominant member of the family.

This approach is put forward most forcibly by the Dobashes in their study of 109 wives who were the subjects of assaults by their husbands. There are three strands to the argument:

Historical. Throughout history, the use of violence by husbands has been culturally acceptable and even the law has seemed to accept that a certain level of violence was justifiable for a husband to maintain discipline within the family.

Cultural. In contemporary British society, the family is an unequal institution in which the male receives most benefit and where he is expected to be dominant. The use of coercion is acceptable, if the wife fails to perform her 'duties' adequately. Women are socialised throughout childhood into the correct behaviour expected of them in marriage, as good mothers and wives. Men, too, are raised with high expectations of the wife/mother role. There is far less stress in our culture on the domestic duties of husband.

Specific factors. The Dobashes, and also Pahl, argue that specific factors may spark-off violence—these can include: disputes over money; jealousy on the part of the husband; or drunkenness. However, these can only lead to violence when there is a cultural 'context' which says that one way to resolve these problems for the male is to assault the female.

Anyway, I was very tired that night and I went to bed early. Then he came to bed, and my little girl woke up, because she'd wet the bed. Anyway I went to see to her and I took the sheet and I moved it round so that I moved her off the wet part. And I went back to bed. Anyway she cried again and he went out to see to her. And I didn't know what had hit me. He came in and he ripped the clothes off me and grabbed me by the feet, and dragged me out of bed. And he kicked me out into the hall and he called me all these names, and he said, "How dare you leave that child with a wet sheet on the bed." And he threw me into her bedroom. So I did the little girl, changed the bed all right round again, and then I went into the bathroom and locked the door, because I was so upset. He came in and knocked the bolt off and he dragged me back into our bedroom to make the bed. And I remember I had my dressing gown on and he threw me all the way down the hall and he ripped my dressing gown and then he threw me on the floor and he was kicking me and I was sitting there screaming. And then he said he'd give me half and hour and then I was to go back into the bedroom and I was to apologise and he meant apologise properly. He put one arm round my throat, and he slapped me and punched me and he said, "How dare you look at me as if I'm repulsive to you. You're my wife, and I'll do what the bloody hell I like to you".

Source: Pahl, *Marital Violence and Public Policy*, Routledge and Kegan Paul, 1985

☐ 1 **This extract suggests that the motivation of the husband was closely related to the husband's definition of:**
   (a) his role,
   (b) a wife and mother's role.
   Could you explain this?
2 **Which explanation(s) for marital violence does this extract support?**

☐ **ESSAYS**
   1 **The most common victims of crime are male, Why then is there so much concern over *women* as victims of crime?**
   2 **Assess the competing explanations for rape.**
   3 **Convictions for violence against wives are very low. Why then are feminist sociologists pariculary interested in this area?**

Bibliography

M. Hough and P. Mayhew, *The British Crime Survey*, HMSO, 1983

F. Clemente and M. Kleinman, *Fear of Crime in the United States*, in Social Forces Magazine, 1977

R. Kinsey, *Merseyside Crime Survey*, Merseyside Metropolitan Council, 1984

J. Lea and J. Young, *What is to be done about Law and Order?*, Penguin, 1984

S. Brownmiller, *Against Our Will*, Secker and Warburg, 1975

C. Smart, *Women, Crime and Criminology—a feminist critique*, RKP, 1978

S. Box, *Crime, Power and Mystification*, Tavistock, 1983

D. Matza, *Delinquency and Drift*, Wiley, 1964

J. Pahl, *Marital Violence and Public Policy*, RKP, 1985

D. Marsden, *Sociological Perspectives on Family Violence*, in J. Martin (ed) *Violence and the Family*, Wiley, 1978

M. Faulk, *Men who Assault Women*, in *Behind Closed Doors: Violence in the American Family*, Anchor Books, 1980

R. Dobash and R. Dobash, *Violence Against Wives*, Open Books, 1979

9 · Crime and the Ethnic Minorities

In recent years, there has been a debate about the relationship of black people and crime. The argument centres on the claim by the police, in particular the Metropolitan Police, that rates of crime for certain street offences are higher amongst young blacks than the population in general. Sociologists have responded in a number of ways to this charge. We will examine these responses in this chapter and also the explanations that have been put forward for criminality amongst blacks in Britain.

Crime rates among ethnic minorities

The Police argument

In its report to the 1972 House of Commons Select Committee on Race Relations, the Metropolitan Police stated that the crime rate amongst black people was approximately the same as, and possibly even lower than, the crime rate for the population as a whole. Furthermore, crime rate amongst Asians was found to be markedly lower than the overall crime rate.

In its evidence to the 1977 Select Committee however, the Metropolitan Police put forward a different view: 12 per cent of those arrested were of 'West Indian or African origin' (35 per cent of those for robbery and violent theft), although they only formed 4.3 per cent of the London population.

The police were aware that the arrest rate was not necessarily an objective measure of black involvement in crime. By using this measure, they were open to criticism, because it could be argued that police officers were racist and were more likely to arrest blacks. They pointed out that for robbery and violent theft (where the criminals were most likely to be seen by the victim), victims identified approximately 36 per cent of assailants as 'coloured'.

In its evidence to *The Scarman Enquiry* following the riots of 1981, the Metropolitan Police stated that, during the years 1976–80, the growth in recorded offences of robbery and other violent theft was 38 per cent for the Metropolitan District as a whole, 66 per cent for 'L' district (which is the general area incorporating Brixton) and 138 per cent for the Brixton subdivision. However, in 'L' District, the overall rise in serious offences was only 13 per cent compared with a general rise of 15 per cent throughout London. The police were, in essence, arguing that Brixton with its high level of people of West Indian origin, contributed disproportionately to the levels of robbery, but not other forms of crime.

Criticisms

The police statistics were criticised on a number of grounds, including:

Age: Most crime is committed by the young. The ethnic minorities have higher proportions of young people than the population as a whole. Therefore, a higher rate of crime could be expected.

Victim bias: Morris argues that white victims are more likely to report crimes against them committed by blacks, than those committed by whites. Morris suggests that this is the result of racial prejudice. It should be noted, however, that the bulk of crime is committed *within* ethnic groups.

Policing patterns: Morris also suggests that as there are more police in inner city areas, where the bulk of black people live, then they are more likely to uncover higher rates of crime.

Police racism: Finally, according to Gilroy, when there was no report by a victim of crime, but where the police were directly involved (ie where a victim had not reported the crime, but the police 'uncovered' one), there were high arrest rates of blacks.

Independent research

In order to find out whether the Metropolitan Police claims were justified or not, the Home Office financed a study by Stevens and Willis (published as *Race, Crime and Arrests,* 1979). This research consisted of two parts: first, a study of the relationship between recorded serious crimes and ethnic minorities in major British cities; and second, a study of the arrest data of the Metropolitan Police.

In their study of British cities, Stevens and Willis concluded that there was absolutely no relationship between the proportions of ethnic minorities and the amount of crime ... 'there is no tendency for areas with high West Indian or Asian proportions to have high recorded indictable crime rates'.

The second part of the study examines the *arrest rates* in the Metropolitan Police District.

First, the authors distinguish between *intrinsic* factors which affect the arrest rate, and *extrinsic* factors.

Intrinsic factors

These consist of the variables of age and socio-economic status.

Arrest rates of whites, Blacks and Asians for indictable crimes

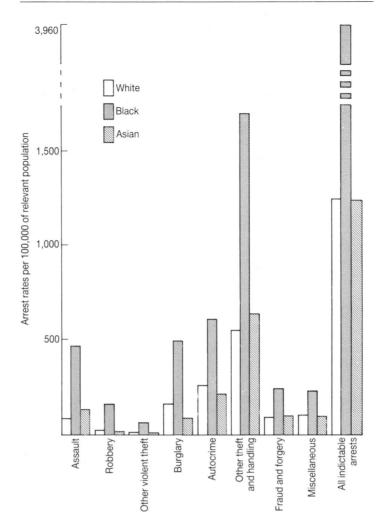

Source: Stevens and Willis, *Race, Crimes and Arrest,* HMSO, 1979

Age. This is important because, as we saw earlier, the vast bulk of crime is committed by young people and the age profile of the ethnic minorities differs from the overall British population, having a greater proportion of young people. However, when Stevens and Willis conducted a statistical test which isolated the age variable, they concluded that the higher arrest rates for blacks in the Metropolitan Police District could not be explained by the age profile while for Asians the arrest rates should actually have been higher.

Socio-economic status. Next, Stevens and Willis compared crime rates and ethnic groups for all twenty-two of the Metropolitan Police Districts against such factors as unemployment, household tenure and membership of 'socio-economic groups' (social class). Black, white and Asian arrest rates were all directly associated with social deprivation, but different factors seemed to affect the various ethnic groups differently.

Extrinsic factors

By extrinsic factors, Stevens and Willis mean *differential law enforcement* by the police.

First, they found little difference in the amount of crime being *reported* to the police between the ethnic groups, and most of these crimes according to the victims were *intra-racial*, that is white on white and black on black. When it came to arrest rates, they found that although there might very well be racial prejudice in the activities of the police, this alone could not explain the police arrest rates. For example, if all the differences in the arrest rates were a result of police activity alone, it would have meant that 66 per cent of all black offenders would have been arrested and only 21 per cent of white offenders. (These figures are obtained by comparing the ethnic origin of the offender according to the victim with the arrest rates of the police.) This seems too great a disparity to be true.

A further strengthening of the argument that the higher crime rate of blacks cannot be explained by differential policing, is that 92 per cent of all recorded serious crimes are reported directly by victims—only 8 per cent are initiated by the police. This means that the police can only influence a very small proportion of crimes reported.

The role of the police in creating crime statistics—critical approaches

A number of sociologists however have continued to be critical of the police, and argue that the criminal statistics are partly a result of police activity. However, these critics vary widely in their approaches.

The racist State

Since the mid–1970s, dating from the publication of *Policing the Crisis* by Hall *et al*, one influential strand of Marxist sociology has argued that the high arrest rate for blacks in inner cities is the result of deliberate police activity. More recently, this argument has been taken up by sociologists of the Centre for Contemporary Cultural Studies in *The Empire Strikes Back*, who claim that the police and the British State are racist and are pursuing a deliberate policy of oppression against blacks.

According to these sociologists, during the early 1970s the press began to concentrate on a new type of street crime—termed 'mugging'. Intense political and media pressure led to a much stricter style of policing in the Brixton area of London, where most of the mugging was reputed to take place. The media, fed by police reports, focused the blame for the muggings on black youths. The new style policing consisted of aggressive 'stop and search' operations, conducted by groups of police officers who were especially brought in for these operations. The result, according to Hall, was that arrests rose not because the muggers were being caught, but because the police were arresting large numbers of black youths as a result of their prejudiced stereotypes.

Hall went on to claim that the police presence was not really an attempt to control mugging, but a response by the State to the threat to its authority posed by young blacks in general. The issue of mugging was merely *justification* for the introduction of much more repressive, aggressive policing policies in inner city areas.

For example, in 1981, during operation 'Swamp 81', in which Brixton was the target of a huge police operation of 'stop and search', over 1,000 people were stopped and searched, yet less than 100 people were charged with any offence. The majority of these offences (eg. obstruction) were directly the result of the police presence and would not have occurred without this.

This general approach has been followed since then by the many Marxist writers, in particular the Race and Politics groups of the Centre for Contemporary Cultural Studies. For example, A. Sivanandan describes the police as: 'a threat, a foreign force, an army of occupation—the thin end of the authoritarian wedge, and in themselves so authoritarian as to make no difference between wedge and state'. (See *From Resistance to Rebellion*, first published in *Race and Class*, Institute of Race Relations, 1981.)

Criticisms

The model of the State as presented by this approach has been criticised because it is too organised and clear-cut in the way it behaves in its defence of capitalism. The idea that the police and top politicians connived to create a 'moral panic' over mugging in order to justify repression of blacks is difficult to accept.

Second, there is little evidence that the police force as an *organisation* is based on racist lines—although some sociologists argue that racism is endemic in the lower ranks of the police, which is a different matter entirely.

Institutionalised racism in the police—the PSI survey

In 1984, PSI (Police Research Institute) conducted a study of the Metropolitan Police at its own request. The study's conclusions were a powerful critique of racism within the lower ranks of the police force. The PSI researchers went on to state that there was a proportion of racist police officers—arguing that racism was a normal part of policing in London. They found that racist language and assumptions underlay all police work, so that terms like 'coon' and 'nigger' were used routinely to describe blacks.

The PSI explanation of police behaviour is that racist attitudes derive from the population in general and as the police are drawn from the wider white population it is to be expected that they will mirror their attitudes. They also point to a 'working culture' which laid heavy emphasis on the criminal nature of blacks.

The PSI research contrasts with the Marxist approach, described earlier, which stresses that the racism of police (which was already present) was directed towards blacks *by the State* as a deliberate part of the battle to control them, rather than an unplanned result of the police officers' working culture.

The police take pride in being a disciplined service so that many policemen obey rules they consider obsolete and suppress their private sentiments. One area car driver told a research worker, "I freely admit that I hate, loathe and despise niggers. I can't stand them. I don't let it affect my job though". The research workers give reasons for believing that people like him succeed in preventing their private feelings from affecting their work. Others, though, may have less self-discipline. According to the study, the degree of tension between the police and black people "was much less than might have been expected either from their own conversation or from accounts in the newspapers and on television". Their conversation indeed was often lurid and racial epithets were frequently used over the personal radio. Such epithets "seem to be more commonly used within the Met than in most other groups: there can be few other groups in which it is normal, automatic, habitual to refer to black people as 'coons', 'niggers', and so on".

The survey found that just over one fifth of Londoners believe that ethnic minority people are unfairly treated by the police. The findings also show that there is far more concern, *among white people as well as among the minorities*, about unfairness towards racial minorities than about unfairness of other kinds. Despite the use of racial epithets, where the victim was a West Indian the police were more likely to take some action, to make a full investigation, to move quickly and to catch the offender, than where the victim was white or Asian. The offender was caught in 22 per cent of the cases where the victim was a West Indian compared with 13 per cent of cases where the victim was white. A similar proportion of West Indians as of white people report victim accidents to the police; a majority of those who do so are satisfied with the service they get, although the level of satisfaction is a little lower than that among white respondents. As regards their willingness to call upon police services and the assessment of the service they receive when they do so, say the PSI, there is no crisis of confidence in the police among West Indians. With the young blacks, though, it is a different story.'

Source: Banton, 'Keeping the Force in Check', *The Times Higher Educational Supplement*, 13 January, 1984

□ 1 **Can private values and work behaviour be separated, in your opinion? You could test this on other occupations (ie. teachers, social workers).**
2 **What does the extract suggest concerning:**
   (a) the attitude of blacks to the police;
   (b) the police response to complaints by the ethnic minorities?

Police tactics and the wider community

The third approach to the police, crime and the ethnic minorities argues that police tactics have actually worsened the crime situation.

In evidence to the *Scarman Commission*, the National Council for Civil Liberties criticised the use of stop and search methods by the police:

> *Even if police officers behaved with impeccable courtesy towards every person stopped and searched and apologised to those found not to be carrying suspect items, many people would resent being treated as suspects when innocently walking to the tube or home.* (Scarman Report)

According to Lea and Young in *What is to be done about Law and Order?* the police do not always behave with 'impeccable politeness' with the result that the black community rejects their authority and refuses to co-operate with them.

In Britain, the vast bulk of arrests by the police occur as a result of information provided by the public. If there is little or no information forthcoming from the public, then the police are forced into a very different style of policing than has been traditional in Britain. In effect, they are forced into behaving like an 'army of occupation', or as Lea and Young term it, *military policing.* This involves random 'stops and searches' in the hope of uncovering information which can lead to arrests. Of course, this further alienates the local community, in particular the older, law-abiding generation. The result is a weakening of the sort of informal social restraints that operate to limit crime in most communities. Indeed, the whole of the black community unite, in certain circumstances, in dislike of the police; so much so that an arrest can easily turn into a confrontation of blacks against the police. Lea and Young term this *mobilisation of bystanders*.

This explanation differs from the view that there is a racist state. Lea and Young accept that there really are higher levels of crime committed by blacks. This fuels police racism which is already present and starts the 'vicious circle' which is described above. On the other hand, the racist state approach argues that it is discrimination by the police which *creates* a high arrest rate of blacks.

The process is described in the diagram below.

The effects of Military policing

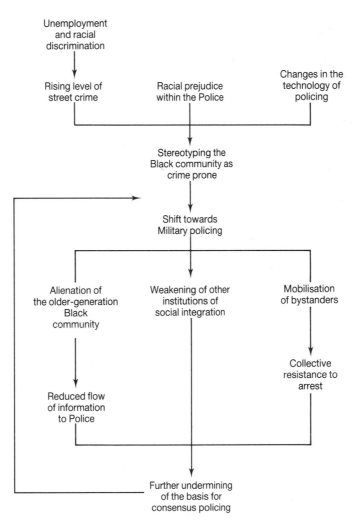

Source: Lea and Young, *What is to be done about Law and Order?*, Penguin, 1984

Criticisms

Central to the Lea and Young model are the arguments that (a) the police are actually discriminatory in their dealings with young blacks, and (b) the black community is aware of this.

However, the PSI study indicated that the police were trying to distinguish between their own racism and their duty as police officers (how far they are successful in that was not researched in the study) and they noted that police officers were *more likely* to take seriously a report of a criminal offence against blacks than against whites.

Lea and Young's arguments are partially supported by the work of Gaskill and Smith in their 1983 study of the attitudes of blacks to the police, *How Young Blacks see the Police.* Only 30 per cent of young blacks were likely to hold the view that the police were 'good' or 'very good', compared to 60 per cent of young whites. They also found that the black community's negative views of the police were held irrespective of their own experience of the police (that is, even if the police had been polite, they were still viewed with distrust). However, Gaskill and Smith found that the stop and search rates were virtually *equal* for young blacks and young whites in inner city areas.

Finally, even if blacks have less faith in the police than whites, all available research indicates that they have similar rates of reporting crime to the police as the rest of the community. This would not fit into any of the above models of police/ethnic minority relations.

Ezaz Hayat bought a fast food shop in Canning Town 15 months ago. Immediately, he was visited by a teenage gang called the Croydon Road Boys who told him he was in 'a white man's area' and that they didn't want coloured people there. In September last year, a member of Ezaz's staff was punched in the face and shortly afterwards there was a petrol bomb attack on the shop. In November, Ezaz's brother-in-law and his teenage son were beaten semi-conscious outside the shop by a large gang of white youths, one of whom shouted 'kill the Paki'.

Following pressure from the Newham Monitoring Group and the council, the police arrested seven people, five of whom were charged, taken to court, but acquitted. Both Ezaz and the Monitoring Group allege that this was because the police had prepared the case badly. The police did not consult Ezaz even though he was a major prosecution witness. 'I never heard from them and they never made any inquiries in the neighbourhood', he said. 'They called me up the day before the trial and told me to be in court.'

The exact scale of the problem is difficult to determine, since many attacks are not reported. Last year, police figures listed 1,481 for the entire London metropolitan area. This year, police figures for the first quarter showed a slight increase, to 424. In Newham, however, which has an Asian population of over 40 per cent, the June figures found a 100 per cent increase compared with last year, with 188 reported incidents.

Police attribute this dramatic increase to a major publicity campaign launched in January this year in Newham, giving practical information on racial harassment and encouraging people to report incidents to the police.

The Harris report, an independent survey commissioned by Newham Council from the Harris Research Centre published in March, indicated that the scale of racial harassment may be greater than police statistics have shown. The survey, the first of its kind, interviewed 1,063 black residents of Newham. It concluded that one in four of Newham's black residents had been subject to some form of racial harassment in the previous 12 months, that only one in 20 of these had been reported to the police, and that 80 per cent who had gone to the police were dissatisfied with the way their case had subsequently been handled.

The police argue that it is often difficult to find concrete evidence and even that some black families may be deliberately using the issue of racial harassment as an 'excuse' to get on the housing transfer list.

One solicitor with wide experience of racial harassment cases told me: 'The courts and the police are generally reluctant to admit a racial element. If there's a fight and a black family rings up, the police will often talk first to the white family and treat the victim as a suspect.'

In answer to their critics, police claim to have a higher clear-up rate for racial harassment cases than for other crimes such as burglary. But the police definition of a clear-up may simply mean that the incident has been recorded as a neighbourhood dispute and referred to another agency such as the housing authority. Out of 114 reported clear-ups, between January and March this year, police figures show 45 arrests, but it is not recorded how many of these were taken to court.

Most racial harassment cases fall into the legal category of common assault and actual bodily harm. Although the police are obliged to prosecute for actual bodily harm, the decision to prosecute for common assault is optional.

There is clearly a widely held view among many black East Enders that the police are indifferent, if not overtly hostile to their interests. This distrust extends to the political and administrative machinery of white society.

Stuart Goodwin, the police Press liaison officer for Newham, denied such allegations. 'We don't pretend to be perfect, but we're doing the best we can. There is a perception on some people's part that racial harassment is the police's fault, but at the end of the day we can't change people's prejudices. It's part of life.'

Source: The Observer, 'Racism's Short Fuse' article, 22 November, 1987

□ **PROJECT**

Some sociologists argue that the Race and Crime debate has become a distraction from the REAL issue of racial attacks.
(You may find this extract particularly interesting if you have already read the chapter on crime statistics.)
What evidence is there to show that official statistics of racially-motivated crime may be inaccurate?
Explain this in terms of: a) the role of the police; b) the role of the black and Asian communities; c) the role of other agencies.

Explanations for crime amongst the ethnic minorities

The race and politics collective approach

In *The Empire Strikes Back*, a collection of papers by the Race and Politics Collective, including Gilroy and Bridges, the authors argue that crime amongst blacks is a reflection of the continuing struggle between the 'colonial' powers represented by the police on the one hand and the local black communities on the other.

Their argument is that the best way to examine the situation of blacks in Britain is to see it in the context of colonialism. In the late eighteenth century, and throughout the nineteenth century, Britain dominated the world by acquiring colonies by military might. The countries were then exploited for their mineral and agricultural wealth, while the population was initially forced into slavery and later into (starvation level) wage labourers.

There was a continual need for the British to keep control over a conquered local colonial population and this was done through a mixture of brute force and 'education'.

The history of colonialism, therefore, contained a strong element of repression by the colonial authorities. The colonial 'nations' responded to their conquest in a variety of ways which expressed their hostility, occasionally breaking into outright rebellion.

Independence movements were portrayed by the British in terms of criminality—for example, the Mau-Mau rebellion in Kenya in the 1950s led by Kenyatta, which the British saw as an example of cruel lawlessness.

Towards the end of the British Empire, after the Second World War, the British economy was being rebuilt and there was a desperate need for labour. As a result, immigrant labour, primarily West Indian, from the colonies was encouraged to come to Britain. Africans had been shipped to the West Indies in the eighteenth century to work as slaves on the sugar and tobacco plantations. By the 1950s, low wages and high unemployment were characteristic of life in the West Indies. There was nothing 'natural' about this, rather it was the result of the economic and social structure created by the British. Immigration to Britain was therefore a direct result of colonialism. Once they arrived in Britain, they were faced by racial hostility and suffered in terms of poor housing, low-paid jobs and exclusion from British social life.

According to the *Race and Politics Collective*, the conditions of the colonies were, therefore, reproduced here in Britain in the inner city ethnic communities. Black crime represents the continuation of the struggle of the blacks against 'colonialism' transferred from the original colonies back into the 'motherland' itself. The activities of the young blacks represent to them a form of rebellion; to the police and the State their activities are simply criminal.

According to this model, black people have developed quite distinctive, oppositional subcultures to the main society, which derive from their history of oppression. Crime represents a form of '*organised resistance*' to the authorities, which draws upon the traditions of the anti-colonial struggle. The key point here is that the blacks' 'criminality' is viewed from this perspective as a form of *politics*, which may not be recognisable to the outsider, but is nevertheless essentially a political struggle against oppression. The unusual political form derives from the fact that black people have been excluded from organised political structures in Britain (the main political parties and the Trades Unions); and second, because this form of political struggle derives from colonial oppression, which white British commentators have never suffered.

Criticisms

There are a number of discrepancies in this account of crime amongst blacks. The first of these is that until recently there appears to have been particularly low rates of crime amongst West Indians in Britain. The high crime rate only appears with the second (and third) generations of black people. If crime is part of the anti-colonial struggle, why was (and still is) the first generation so law-abiding?

The second problem concerns the way in which the authors argue that black people commit crime as a form of political struggle. There is simply no evidence to support a widespread awareness of this amongst black youth. Indeed, the evidence suggests that black youth by and large subscribe to the general values and aspirations of the wider society. Rather than being in opposition, they appear conformist (apart from their view on the police). One must be suspicious when 'experts' can read meaning into behaviour that the actual participants are totally unaware of.

Subculture: resistance through rituals

A related approach to the one discussed above stresses the development of youth subcultures as a form of resistance to capitalism. This has been discussed on pages 79–83, here it will be applied to the responses of black people.

You will recall that, according to the Marxist subcultural approach, youth form the weakest link in the control of the working class by the rich, as they are not yet locked into the system through mortages, families and fixed employment. In response to the situation in which they find themselves, they develop 'magical' solutions via youth subcultures.

Black youth are no exception to this and have developed a number of different responses, reflecting their particular position in the British social structure. A clear example is the adoption of *Rastafarian* beliefs by many young blacks. In the 1920s Marcus Garvey, a prominent black figure who lived in the USA and later Jamaica, argued that blacks ought to return to Africa and that a black king would be crowned as the redeemer. When Haile Selassie was crowned in 1930, it seemed that Marcus' prophecy had come true. The religion took on the name *Rastafarianism* because Haile Selassie's name before being crowned was *Ras Tafari.*

Rastafarians in Jamaica believe that the human body is of little importance; instead Rastafarians should attempt to reach a higher spiritual plain. Ignoring their bodies can mean not washing and leaving their hair to grow—hence the hairstyle which is a feature of Rastafarianism. Marihuana is routinely smoked because it induces a higher spiritual state whereby the person is removed from the cares of everyday life. Rastas wear green and gold colours, the national colours of Ethiopia. Rastafarianism amongst British black youth can be viewed as reaction to a society which denies blacks any cultural identity. It provides a unique cultural heritage which distinguishes them from whites (indeed it is exclusive to blacks) and gives them pride.

Of course, Rastafarianism is not illegal (although using marihuana is). However, in terms of the dominant white culture the style of dress and the central ideas are certainly deviant. More importantly to sociologists who subscribe to the Marxist subcultural school, the development of alternative subcultures showed how the young blacks were 'resisting' the dominant hegemony (set of values) of capitalism and were indeed fighting back.

Rastafarianism was not the only form of resistance shown by young blacks; other deviant and illegal responses emerged. For example, Friend and Metcalfe comment that:

> *black neighbourhoods opened up the possibility of surviving by alternative means, by a process of hustling involving activities such as gambling, undeclared part-time work, ganja (marihuana) selling, shoplifting, street crime, housebreaking and distributing stolen goods.* (Friend and Metcalfe, *Slump City*, Pluto, 1981)

Criticisms

This explanation has also been criticised for focusing on the few deviant and illegal subcultures of black youth. There is a much wider variety of responses than the 'oppositional' ones put forward by the Marxist subcultural school. For example, some conformist and some deviant responses, which Ken Pryce describes in detail in *Endless Pressure*, a study of blacks in Bristol.

A further criticism is, as we discussed earlier, can sociologists justify their explanations when the participants themselves may not agree with these? Rastafarians do not see themselves as 'resisting capitalism'.

Varieties of Blacks' responses to their position in British society

Adapted from Pryce, *Endless Pressure*, Penguin, 1979

Anomie and marginalisation

A third approach to race and crime, stresses the way that blacks have been effectively *marginalised* from white society and in response they have turned to crime. This approach uses a modified version of Merton's concept of *anomie*, which you will remember argues that when a society stresses the importance of achieving financial success and the possession of consumer items, yet fails to provide people with any realistic chances of obtaining these goals legally, then some people will turn to crime to achieve the desired financial success. This argument has been put forward most noticeably by Cashmore in *No Future*. He portrays young blacks in Britain trapped in a situation where their aspirations and the reality of their economic situation do not match.

In contemporary British society status is partially measured in terms of material possessions, and young black people are as likely as any other young people to want cars, stereos, smart clothes, etc. The desire for possessions is fuelled by advertising and by a culture that seems to state 'you are what you own'. With particularly high levels of youth unemployment amongst blacks, up to 50 per cent in inner city areas, they will spend large parts of each day simply congregating in city centre areas. Here they are surrounded by the consumer goods they

☐ **Can the concept of anomie be applied to young blacks? Find evidence to prove or disprove the argument that blacks experience greater obstacles to success in British society. You should examine in particular the evidence relating to education, type of employment, unemployment, housing, experience of discrimination, and policing. The infomation can be found in most of the major textbooks on race, as well as in back copies of *The New Statesman* and *New Society.* For detailed project work you should write to the Commission for Racial Equality.**

want—a constant temptation. The outcome is that they are drawn into crime.

This model differs from Merton's use of anomie in that there is no attempt to look at the different responses to a situation of anomie (see diagram p. 18), and, second, Cashmore specifically comments on the young blacks' awareness that much of their marginality is a result of *being* black and living in 'a world of Babylon', which exploits and degrades them. Their criminal activities are justified on the grounds that Babylon (the white society) has given them nothing, so why should they follow its laws?

Criticism

The modified version of *anomie* fails to account for the variety of responses amongst young blacks. Why is it that only a small proportion of young blacks engage in crime, if they are all faced by similar 'blocks' against success?

The left realist approach

In *What is to be done about Law and Order?* Lea and Young apply their model of 'new realism'. They suggest that there are three elements to an understanding of crime and the ethnic minorities: marginality, relative deprivation and subculture.

Marginality

Young blacks tend to be less successful in the education system; to have particularly high levels of unemployment; and when they are employed to be in lower-paid jobs; to have few means of political expression. Lea and Young claim that as a result of this, young blacks occupy a position on the edges of British society.

Relative deprivation

Whereas most other explanations of black crime stress the differences in the values of white and black youth, Lea and Young argue that it is precisely the similarities between black youth and the rest of the society that causes the trouble. They claim that the culture of young blacks is distinct from that of the older generation and derives more from the expectations and aspirations of British society than from any hangover from West Indian society. It is precisely this *similarity* which causes much of the crime. Black youth have particularly high aspirations compared with their parents, for material goods and styles of life—yet the reality of their life in Britain is one where they are unlikely legally to achieve these aspirations.

Subculture

Lea and Young suggest that young blacks respond differently to the mismatch between aspirations and the constraints of reality, and that there is no automatic move towards crime, as Cashmore seems to suggest. They argue that one of a *number* of responses has been the drift to petty crime by some blacks.

Crime amongst other ethnic minorities

What is particularly noticeable in any discussion of crime rates is the absence of detailed discussions on the Indians, Pakistanis, and Chinese. In the case of the Chinese, this reflects a blindspot in British society in general towards this group. Suffice it to say that the conviction rates for Chinese are extremely low. This could be partially explained by the 'closed' nature of Chinese society in Britain and the fact that few crimes are reported to the police by the community, which prefers to sort out its own problems. It is interesting that where Chinese are convicted of violent crimes, for example, it tends to be the result of a fight between Chinese and non-Chinese, where the police are subsequently called in by outsiders.

In the case of Indians and Pakistanis, the levels of convictions are also low. Various explanations have been suggested, some of which could also be applied to the Chinese:

Greater economic success. Indians in particular have been successful in business and seem more likely to be in employment than black people. Therefore, they suffer less from the marginality experienced by young blacks.

Stronger family and community. Asian families are particularly strong and impose strict controls over family members. As in the situation of white females, strict socialisation and control of social activities of Asian youth may limit the opportunities (and possibly the interest) in deviant activities.

Distinct culture. One of the key points made by Lea and Young was that black crime rates are high because young blacks embrace British culture and are, therefore, more likely to be bitter when they fail. Asian cultures are more distinct, providing a clear alternative to the mainstream British culture. Asians are, therefore, less likely to feel marginalised or to suffer from relative deprivation.

☐ ESSAYS

1 **There is considerable dispute over the extent to which young blacks are involved in street crime. Explain the reasons for this dispute and assess the respective arguments.**
2 **Critically assess the explanations sociologists have proposed for the crimes committed by young blacks.**

Bibliography

Lord Scarman, *The Scarman Report*, Penguin, 1982
T. Morris, *Submission to the Commission for Racial Equality*, quoted in *What is to be done about Law and Order?*, by J. Lea and J. Young, Penguin, 1984
P. Stevens and C. Willis, *Race, Crimes and Arrests*, HMSO, 1979
P. Gilroy, *The Myth of Black Criminality* in the Socialist Register magazine, Merlin Press, 1982 pp 47–56
S. Hall *et al*, *Policing the Crisis*, Macmillan, 1979

Centre for Contemporary Cultural Studies, *The Empire Strikes Back*, Hutchinson, 1983
L. Bridges and P. Gilroy, *Striking Back*, Marxism Today pp 34–35, 1982
A. Sivanandan, *From Resistance to Rebellion: Race and Class* pp 11–152, Institute of Race Relations, 1981
K. Pryce, *Endless Pressure*, Penguin, 1979
A. Friend and A. Metcalfe, *Slump City*, Pluto, 1981
E. Cashmore, *No Future*, Heinemann, 1984

The validity of statistics

Each year the Home Office releases statistics showing the changes in the crime rate, an example of which is shown below. The statistics purport to show the changing patterns of crime, for example how many burglaries or crimes of violence have taken place. These are used for a number of purposes. For example:

they can be compared with previous years to see how the overall trends in crime are moving,

they can be compared with the police 'clear-up' rate, to work out an index of police efficiency,

they can be used to work out where the police should concentrate their resources,

they provide the public (often via the newspapers) with the information on the sorts of people committing crimes, and in what circumstances and places they commit them.

Some sociologists base their explanations of crime on them.

We can see then that these crime statistics provide an important source of knowledge for the public, the police and sociologists. As a result of the information provided an image of typical criminals and typical crimes has been developed. This tells us that criminals are generally:

male,

under the age of 25,

working class,

those of West Indian origin have higher than expected levels of crime, given their proportion in the population.

Numbers cautioned or found guilty of indictable offences

Numbers of notifiable crimes known to the Police in England and Wales

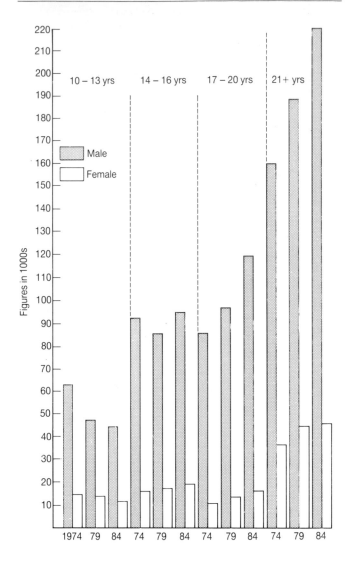

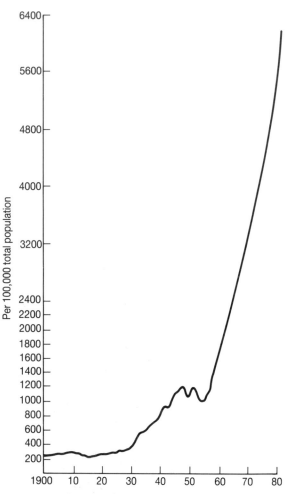

Source: Updated from *Crime in England and Wales*, Heinemann, 1968

☐ **Using *Social Trends*, update the figures in the diagrams above.**

However, most sociologists since the 1960s have regarded the official statistics with some considerable doubt. Attacks on the reliability of the official statistics came from a variety of directions. Sociologists all shared the belief that the statistics said more about the process of reporting (by the public) and collating (by the police and judiciary) of acts which came to be *defined* as criminal, than about the numbers of criminal acts themselves. Furthermore, the argument ran, if the 'real' crime rate was ever uncovered then the categories of 'typical criminals' as described above would be viewed as completely incorrect.

It was in response to these sorts of concerns that sociologists developed two techniques to uncover the true picture of crime. These were *self-report studies* and *victimisation surveys.*

Self-report studies

These consist of confidential questionnaires in which respondents are asked to record whether they have committed any of the criminal acts which are listed. These have revealed that criminal acts are spread throughout the population and that the official differences between males and females or working and middle class are far smaller than the official statistics would suggest. For both sets of comparisons, the official statistics record a six to one difference in criminal acts committed (ie. male to female; working to middle class), yet, self-report studies reveal that the ratios tumble to about three to two. The importance of these revelations is that many sociologists have started with the assumption that the ratios provided by the official statistics are correct, and therefore base their entire theories on them. If the statistics are incorrect it may well be that the theories are incorrect.

Before we accept this dramatic conclusion, we should be aware that there are a number of severe criticisms of self-report studies. According to Box (*Deviance, Reality and Society*) these can be centred around the issues of *validity*, *relevance* and *representativeness*.

Validity. To what extent are the replies given in the self-report tests true to reality? Self-report studies have most often been used with adolescents, because it is they who commit most crime (and, I suspect, it is easy for researchers to administer the questionnaires to students!). It has been argued that working class youths may be particularly wary of admitting crime to middle class representatives of authority, such as University researchers; on the other hand, middle class youths may feel relaxed and cheerfully own up to everything. Of course, we could also suggest that both middle and working class youths may feel the wish to exaggerate in order to impress their peer group (remembering that these questionnaires are often given out in school). Take your pick of the above explanations; they all suggest that the self-report studies do not get at the 'truth'. An attempt to entangle all these was made by Gold, who used a combination of self-report studies and intensive interviewing. Gold's conclusion was that about 80 per cent of those being interviewed were telling the truth.

Relevance. The second criticism of self-report studies has been that they list so many trivial items it is no wonder that the differences between the various social classes are minimised, after all *everybody* commits some tiny infraction of the law at some time. Furthermore, some studies have included acts of deviance which are not even illegal, such as 'defying parents' authority'. The outcome is that the studies are not really measuring significant infractions of the law, but trivial acts that are widespread among the population.

Representativeness. Earlier, it was mentioned that the majority of self-report studies were given to adolescents in schools. This is useful for *delinquency,* but tells us little about serious *adult* infractions of the law—in particular, the extent of white-collar crime.

An example of a self-report study

Acts of delinquency

1 I have ridden a bicycle without lights after dark.
2 I have driven a car or motor bike/scooter under 16.
3 I have been with a group who go round together making a row and sometimes getting into fights and causing a disturbance.
4 I have played truant from school.
5 I have travelled on a train or bus without a ticket or deliberately paid the wrong fare.
6 I have let off fireworks in the street.

7   I have taken money from home without returning it.

8   I have taken someone else's car or motor bike for a joy ride then taken it back afterwards.

9   I have broken or smashed things in public places like on the streets, cinemas, dance halls, trains or buses.

10 I have insulted people on the street or got them angry and fought with them.

11 I have broken into a big store or garage or warehouse.

12 I have broken into a little shop even though I may not have taken anything.

13 I have taken something out of a car.

14 I have taken a weapon (like a knife) out with me in case I needed it in a fight.

15 I have fought with someone in a public place like in the street or a dance.

16 I have broken the window of an empty house.

17 I have used a weapon in a fight, like a knife or a razor or a broken bottle.

18 I have drunk alcoholic drinks in a pub under 16.

19 I have been in a pub when I was under 16.

20 I have taken things from big stores or supermarkets when the shop was open.

21 I have taken things from little shops when the shop was open.

22 I have dropped things in the street like litter or broken bottles.

23 I have bought something cheap or accepted as a present something I knew was stolen.

24 I have planned well in advance to get into a house to take things.

25 I have got into a house and taken things even though I didn't plan it in advance.

26 I have taken a bicycle belonging to someone else and kept it.

27 I have struggled or fought to get away from a policeman.

28 I have struggled or fought with a policeman who was trying to arrest someone.

29 I have stolen school property worth more than about 5p.

30 I have stolen goods from someone I worked for worth more than about 5p.

31 I have had sex with a boy when I was under 16.

32 I have trespassed somewhere I was not supposed to go, like empty houses, railway lines or private gardens.

33 I have been to an 'X' film under age.

34 I have spent money on gambling under 16.

35 I have smoked cigarettes under 15.

36 I have had sex with someone for money.

37 I have taken money from slot machines or telephones.

38 I have taken money from someone's clothes hanging up somewhere.

39 I have got money from someone by pretending to be someone else or lying about why I needed it.

40 I have taken someone's clothing hanging up somewhere.

41 I have smoked dope or taken pills (LSD, mandies, sleepers).

42 I have got money/drink/cigarettes by saying I would have sex with someone even though I didn't.

43 I have run away from home.

Source: Campbell, *Girl Delinquents*, Blackwell, 1981

☐ **PROJECT**

Carry out a self-report study. Make sure you organise it so that people can take part anonymously.

☐ **The questions above are taken from three self-report studies and show typical questions used in studying young people.**
1. **Examine the questions—do you think they accurately measure deviance?**
2   **If you think the questions could be bettered, alter or replace them.**

Victimisation surveys

An alternative approach for discovering the true extent of the statistics is to ask people which crimes had been committed against them in the last year. The argument is that, with certain exceptions, people are more likely to provide researchers with crimes committed against them, rather than crimes they have committed against others and are therefore guilty of.

The method was first developed in the USA by the President's Commission on Law Enforcement and Administration of Justice. Surveys were conducted on people living in Washington, Chicago and Boston, and the results were quite staggering. For example, personal injury crime was twice the official rate, and property crime, excluding burglary, was three times higher than the official rate.

In Britain, this has resulted in the development of *The British Crime Surveys*, carried out in 1981 and 1983. These consisted of asking one person over sixteen in 11,000 households: (a) whether they had been victims of a crime in the previous year; and (b) whether they had reported them to the police; and (c) whether the police had recorded them.

The *Surveys* revealed a staggering gap between the amount of crime committed and that finally recorded by the police. This is illustrated in the diagram below.

Levels of recorded and unrecorded crime, 1983

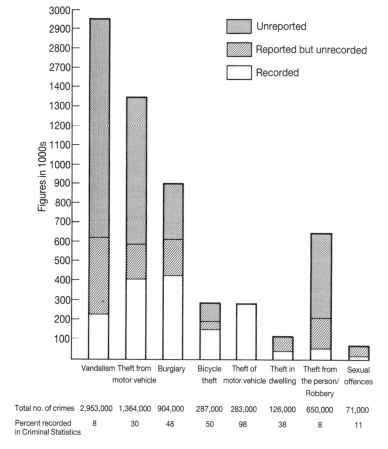

	Vandalism	Theft from motor vehicle	Burglary	Bicycle theft	Theft of motor vehicle	Theft in dwelling	Theft from the person/ Robbery	Sexual offences
Total no. of crimes	2,953,000	1,364,000	904,000	287,000	283,000	126,000	650,000	71,000
Percent recorded in Criminal Statistics	8	30	48	50	98	38	8	11

Source: British Crime Survey, HMSO, 1985

Reporting of crime

Only 22 per cent of acts of vandalism were reported, 18 per cent of cases of theft from a dwelling, and just over half the cases of violent assault! Indeed, of the categories of crime asked about in the survey (see diagram above) only 34 per cent of the total were reported to the police.

Recording of crime

When it came to the recording of crime by the police, only 8 per cent of theft and vandalism, 11 per cent of sexual offences and 48 per cent of burglaries eventually entered the official records.

Victims

The common image of the victims of crime was found to be false too. The middle-aged, the affluent and females were *not* victims, but young, working class males were. (Although *The Islington Crime Survey* (see page 105) found that women *were* significantly more likely to be the victims of non-sexual attacks than men.) Victims were also found to be concentrated in inner city areas. We ought to note though that females may well not often be the victims of crime because they rarely venture out at night for fear of assault.

The *British Crime Surveys* indicate a massive under-reporting and under-recording of crime, but there is evidence to suggest that even the surveys under-record the true extent of crime. Kinsey, Lea and Young (see *Losing the Fight against Crime*) have suggested a number of weaknesses in the *Surveys*. In particular, they do not record any crimes relating to drugs, prostitution or white-collar crime. Also, they do not include crimes of which people are unaware, such as tax evasion or corporation crime.

Furthermore, many women are still not prepared to report sexual offences committed against them, even in the confidentiality of the survey. The *Surveys* rely on people's memories, and of course many minor criminal acts may be forgotten, or regarded as not serious enough to record. Finally, the *Surveys* rely upon peoples' ability to classify acts as crimes, and there is clearly considerable room for misunderstanding here.

The *Surveys* have had considerable influence on policy in Britain. They show that crime is committed against quite specific groups of people—mainly young and male, in specific areas, mainly inner city and adjoining zones. They also show that those people who were not in the 'high risk' groups were unlikely to be victims. For example, the statistically 'average' person could expect a robbery once every five centuries, a burglary once every forty years and an assault once every century. As most crime is petty and we know that the chances of being caught are minimal, current policing practices appear to have little effect on the crime rates. More police do not mean less crime.

Factors affecting the reporting and recording of criminal statistics

In this section, we will examine why the rate of reporting and recording of crime is so low. The reasons are complex and intertwined, therefore it would be clearest to untangle them under the following topics:

The public's reporting of crime,
Invisible crime,
The police,
The judiciary,
The media,
Political pressures.

Influences on the public's reporting of crime

Before we begin the discussion, it should be pointed out that less than 10 per cent of crime is directly observed or uncovered by the police. The remaining 90 per cent comes from complaints from the public. The main findings of the *British Crime Surveys* concerning the reporting of crime to the police were that:

(a) People do not report crimes which they define as too petty, or which they believe the police will define as trivial.

(b) People report crimes when there is an advantage in it for them. Thus, 98 per cent of thefts of motor cars were reported to the police, presumably because they were insured.

(c) Some crimes are regarded as private matters to be settled between individuals.

(d) The victim may not want to harm the offender—this is particularly important in intra-family crime, for example, the theft of money by a brother.

(e) Victims may be too embarrassed to complain to the police. This seems particularly important in the case of sexual offences, where the police are perceived as uncaring, and the procedures for dealing with rape victims appear humiliating. Estimates of the true extent of rape are unreliable, but even the *British Crime Surveys*, which certainly under-represents the true level of rape, suggests that the real level is two and a half times the official one.

(f) The victim may be unable to inform, at the very worst he/she may be dead!

In *Losing the Fight against Crime*, Kinsey, Lea and Young have developed a model of the relationship between the local communities and the police, which they claim explains why inner city communities are unwilling to report crimes to the police or to assist police officers. They argue that:

(a) Inner city communities have little faith in the police, believing that they are biased against them. For instance in the *Merseyside Crime Survey* (a large scale study of the police and crime patterns around Liverpool), overall 30 per cent of respondents expressed a lack of belief in police fairness. This inhibits them from informing the police, if there is no direct benefit to them from doing so (as discussed in (a) earlier).

(b) Respondents in inner city areas were reluctant to report cases of street crime to the police, for fear of reprisals by the criminals. This can be seen to illustrate in a different way, a lack of faith in the police.

(c) The *Merseyside Crime Survey* showed that there was an *inverse relationship between levels of crime and willingness to report crime.* Where there was least crime, that is, in the middle class suburbs around Liverpool, there was the greatest willingness to report crime to the police, but in areas of highest crime levels there was the least willingness to report crime.

This has an important affect on the crime statistics. An illustration of this is the fact that in Granby (a working class district), 21 per cent of the locals had witnessed a theft from a motor car, yet in Ainsdale (an affluent suburb), only 4 per cent had done so. Yet while the people of Ainsdale would report it, a significant proportion of the people of Granby would not.

□ **PROJECT**

Through your local library, the courts and local authority, you can track down the crime statistics for your town.
Find out what categories for crimes and criminals are used. Why are these categories used?
Are there any particular areas of your town which have higher rates of crime than others? Could you offer any explanations for this?
Are there any types of crime which are particularly high? Can you offer any explanations for this?
Devise a questionnaire which asks people which areas in town and what groups of people are most connected with crime, and what sort of crime is committed in your town. Do their replies match the 'facts' you have uncovered. Ask the same questions of the police. Do their replies match the 'facts'?

Invisible crime

Invisible crimes are those of which the victims are generally unaware. These are usually *white-collar crimes*, for example, where an employee regularly embezzles his or her employer—this could be by the routine operation of fiddling travel expenses through to major alterations of the accounting system.

Indeed, in the work of Ditton, *Part-time Crime*, and Mars, *Cheats at Work*, it was discovered that in a large proportion of jobs, theft is seen as a normal way of increasing a wage. Ditton describes how bread salesmen actually gained status from their colleagues for their ability to cheat the shops they delivered to. Salesmen would overcharge, or would maintain the normal price, but reduce the numbers of loaves delivered. They would justify their actions using *techniques of neutralisation* (see Matza, p. 37). For example, large stores would claim that they allowed wastage anyway, so why shouldn't they keep a few loaves back for themselves to sell elsewhere?

Mars describes a wide range of jobs including waiters who routinely steal food and overcharge, regarding these things as not so much illegal (or even immoral), but perks of the job to compensate for low wages. Mars also researched the regular overcharging of customers by garages. These charged the full price for a service, yet did only the minimum amount of work to remain undetected.

There were two things that all these 'fiddles' had in common, First, the customers were rarely aware that they were the victims of crime—hence, the term 'invisible crime'. Second, even when they were caught, punishment was extremely lenient and hardly ever involved calling the police. In the case of a garage or restaurant for example, the customer might get angry or even refuse to pay, but that was the end of the matter.

☐ **Are 'fiddles' *normal*? Is there any way you can find out? Discuss the alternatives available. Do you think it would be possible for you to research the area of fiddles? (If you think so, do it!)**
If you conclude fiddles are normal, what does this say about traditional 'positivistic' explanations of crime? (See p. 8.)

Corporate crime

We examined the issue of corporate crime in detail on pages 73–75, so here are some brief comments concerning its relevance to the criminal statistics.

Corporate crime consists of illegal acts performed by large companies which directly profit the company, rather than directly profiting individuals. A major problem is that the companies are so powerful that they may be able to persuade governments and the public that their actions are not illegal, even if the harm is far greater than all the losses caused by 'street crime' put together.

Even where large companies do break the law in pursuit of profits, they are rarely subject to police investigation—it is likely that they are dealt with through other government agencies or commissions. Carson's classic study of the enforcement of factory safety legislation is a useful example here. When factories were found guilty of breaking the law concerning safety at work, they were usually written to, pointing out that a particular issue 'required attention'. In only 1.5 per cent of all cases where an 'enforcement notice' had been sent (that is, where the company had broken the law) was the company prosecuted.

Of course, the problem of law enforcement becomes even more difficult when the criminals are the government!

The police

The police play a crucial role in deciding which complaints by the public should be categorised as crime, and the acts that should be defined as illegal.

Numbers of serious offences recorded and cleared up by the Metropolitan Police, 1952 – 81

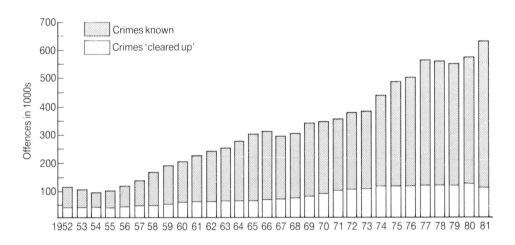

Source: Kinsey, Lea and Young, *Losing the Fight against Crime*, Blackwell, 1986

The police response to the reporting of crime

The overwhelming number of complaints to the police consist of petty crime. Police officers are likely to categorise these acts as crime as much on the social status of the person complaining as on the nature of the act itself. Interestingly, the PSI survey of the Metropolitan Police found that they were *more* likely to respond to a complaint if made by members of the ethnic minorities.

Categorisation of crimes

One of the major influences on the crime statistics is the way that acts are *categorised*. Exactly what distinguishes one crime from another (assault with intent to rob/assault), is unclear. It is up to the police officers themselves to decide the most appropriate category. On that decision rests the fate of the individual (as one category of crime may be far more serious than another), and the construction of the official statistics. The eventual decision by the police officer is usually a result of *police discretion* which we will examine later on.

The construction of the clear-up rate and crimes
'taken into consideration' at the request of the offender

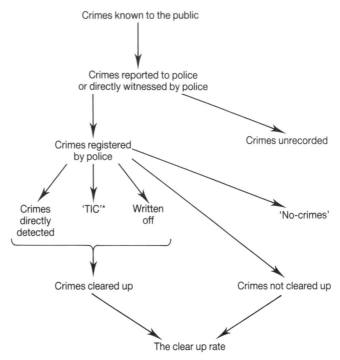

* Crimes 'taken into consideration' at the request of an offender

Source: Ibid.

Dispersal

The police operate with clear ideas of the areas where trouble is most likely to occur, usually in certain inner city areas and large-scale council estates. Therefore, they allocate their officers accordingly. This means that there is a greater likelihood of police officers being aware of offences in these areas.

Routine 'stop and search' may also uncover more crime. However, according to the PSI study, of 1½ million Metropolitan Police 'stops' in 1981, only 8 per cent of those stopped were found to have committed an offence, and only 3 per cent of the total were actually prosecuted! It could be argued that the purpose of 'stops' is to establish police presence and ease police officers' boredom.

Variations in the numbers and type of policing occur between the affluent suburbs and rural areas, and the inner cities. Fewer police are sent to suburbs and the countryside and the style of policing here is likely to be 'consensual', with the officers seeing their role as supporting the community. In inner city areas there are more police, who see their role as *controlling* the local population, in what Lea and Young term a *military policing* role.

Differential enforcement

Police officers in different 'forces' often have different attitudes to

☐ **PROJECT**

Police forces are usually very helpful when asked to help in research. Arrange a day or evening with your local police. Are the points made in this section borne out by the reality of policing?

What problems might occur in researching an organisation such as the police? You may find *Inside the British Police* by Simon Holdaway a particularly interesting book on this subject.

crimes. This reflects the priorities of the senior police officers in the various forces. The significance in terms of the official crime statistics is that concentration by one force on a particular area may generate apparent high levels of 'crime' for a particular offence. Certain forces, for example, are known to be stricter on drink-driving offences, others on prostitution, etc.

The police are noticeably more concerned with 'street crime' than other forms of crime, particularly white-collar or corporate crime, partially through the police definition of 'real policing', which consists of dealing with street crime and the more serious 'physical' forms of crime such as bank/post-office robberies.

Discretion

The most important police influence on the official statistics however, is through their use of *discretion*. This involves police officers using their 'nose' to sense which sort of person is likely to be criminal. The result is that young, working class males, both white and black, are the most likely to be stopped, and it could be argued that this increases the proportion of these in the statistics.

According to a number of studies, including the PSI one, the most important factor when youths are stopped by police is their *demeanour*. If they are co-operative and show respect for police officers they are less likely to be arrested than those who show inadequate respect. In an American study by Piliavin and Briar, only 4 per cent of 'co-operative' youths were arrested, compared to 66 per cent of 'unco-operative'.

Police culture

Understandably enough, most police officers seek promotion. In order to achieve this, they must show adequate arrest rates to their superiors, yet not too many to show up their colleagues, or they will be left out of the close-knit police camaraderie. The resulting balance of arrest rates will influence the total and types of arrests. Furthermore, it is argued that police officers show considerable evidence of racist attitudes, a position supported by the PSI study. It is claimed that this could affect their decision to arrest, although the PSI study found no specific evidence of this.

The smallest increase in the overall crime rate for at least 30 years, coupled with sharp rises in crimes of violence and sex, were announced by the Home Office yesterday.

The 1 per cent increase for 1987 contrasts with figures since the mid-1950s which have shown a constant rise in crime of 6 to 7 per cent. The figure of 3.8 million offences recorded in 1986 rose to 3.9 million in 1987.

A jubilant attitude was prevented by the rises in violence and sex attacks. Mr Hurd said reductions in property crime would allow police to devote time to these areas. The figures show house burglary dropped by 5 per cent, thefts from shops by 3 per cent, thefts of cars dropped by 5 per cent.

Those which increased were robbery, by 8 per cent, sexual offences, by 10 per cent and violence against the person, by 12 per cent.

The number of sexual offences recorded have been increasing for some years because of increased reporting as a result of public concern. Rapes increased by 8 per cent last year, compared with more than 20 per cent in 1985 and 1986. Crime has dropped in the inner city areas with traditionally high crime figures. In Manchester and Merseyside, the drop was 1 per cent, in London 4 per cent and there was no increase in the West Midlands. But rural areas like Gloucestershire and Warwickshire, reported high increases—15 per cent and 11 per cent respectively.

The detection rate, the number of crimes cleared-up

by police, rose by 1 per cent to 33 per cent of all crimes committed. The clear up rate has fallen from 40 per cent in 1980 to 32 per cent in 1986, although the actual number of crimes cleared has risen.

Wide variations exist in detection rates for particular crimes—75 per cent of all violent and sexual offences are solved, but only 23 per cent of thefts of and from cars, which form a quarter of all recorded crime and 26 per cent of house burglaries.

The decrease in cities and increases in rural areas rebutted the argument that crime was caused by deprivation, said Mr Hurd.

Source: Kirby, 'Rise in crime rate of 1% is lowest for at least 30 years', *The Independent,* 26 March, 1988

□ 1. **Why is the increase in the level of crime regarded as a success?**
   2. **Give a breakdown of the various levels of crime by category.**
   3. **What explanation is given for the increase in sexual crimes?**
   4. **What explanations could you offer for the recorded increase in rural crimes?**
   5. **Overall, what comments would you make on all these statistics as a result of the information you have read in this chapter?**

National crime figures, 1987

% changes for England and Wales from 1986

Categories of the 3.9 million crimes recorded in England and Wales in 1987

The judiciary

The role of the police was to act as 'gatekeepers', deciding which acts would be classified as crimes or not. It is from the police figures that the criminal statistics are derived. The influence of the courts is to decide, not what criminal acts have been committed, but if the persons accused are guilty. Nevertheless, it is worth briefly glancing at the work of the courts, as they throw light on the way that the statistics of convictions may also be *manufactured.*

There have been a considerable number of studies on the relationship between racial and social class backgrounds, appearance in court and conviction. However, reviewing the studies in *Crime, Deviance and Mystification,* 1983, Box suggested that the variety of conclusions of the studies indicated that there was 'thin evidence' to suggest that blacks and working class people in court are definitely more likely to be found guilty. These studies miss the point that the overwhelming majority of people who appear in the courts are drawn from lower working class backgrounds (with blacks appearing in much greater numbers than their proportions in the population); and second, that eight out of ten people who appear in court plead guilty. This point is worth looking at in detail.

The British judicial system could not work without the huge majority of the accused pleading guilty. The fact that eight out of ten people appearing in court plead guilty could be an enormous compliment to the British police, but it could also indicate the presence of *plea-bargaining*, which is the practice of offering a person the possibility of a reduction in sentence if they plead guilty. Most of the studies of this have been conducted in the USA, the most interesting being Sudnow's work, *Normal Crimes,* 1972. He found that it was routine to charge an offender with a more serious charge than was warrented and then 'negotiate' with the accused so that he or she pleaded guilty to the offence that the prosecutor really wanted to charge him or her with. In Britain, few studies have been done, but work by Baldwin and McConville who studied 121 Crown Court defendants in Birmingham suggest that plea-bargaining is routine. Even defendants who are resolved to plead not guilty are generally pressured by the *defending* counsel into pleading guilty in the hope of a light sentence. (See *Negotiated Justice,* Martin Robertson, 1977)

Media and political pressures

The last two influences on the construction of criminal statistics are the media and politics. These form the context in which any debate concerning the statistics needs to be understood.

Politics

The role of the state is of particular importance to Marxist writers such as Hall (see p. 71) and Gilroy (see p. 118) who argue that laws are created and enforced against particular sections of the population. The entire edifice of the police and judiciary is there to repress the working class—it is no accident, therefore, that young working class males, both black and white, are heavily over-represented in the prison population. Furthermore, the types of crimes which the police concentrate on, and which form the vast majority of recorded crimes, are those associated with the working class. For them, the absence of corporate and white-collar crime reflects the political structure.

Other writers within the labelling perspective look at the role of politicians in altering the laws, influenced by 'moral entrepreneurs' (see p. 58), or simply public opinion.

The media

The role of the media is discussed fully on pages 62–65. The two main approaches draw from the Marxist and labelling perspectives, both of which stress the *deviance amplifying* nature of the media, through the *sensitising* effects of newspaper and television reports on the activities of various groups.

☐ **Look up the pages referred to in the text above, and construct a chart comparing the Marxist and labelling perspectives on the media and politics. Separately, examine the nature of deviance amplification and the process of police 'sensitising'.**
Take any one example of this process and construct a diagram to illustrate it.

☐ **ESSAYS**
  1 **Why are the sociologists doubtful of the official statistics of crime? Examine the various other ways sociologists use to find out the extent of crime.**
  2 **Examine the way that crime statistics may be said to be 'social constructs'.**
  3 **How can the activities of the police influence the official statistics of crime?**

Bibliography

S. Box, *Deviance, Reality, and Society*, Holt, Rinehart and Winston, 1981

M. Gold, *Undetected Delinquent Behaviour*, in Crime and Delinquency Journal, pp 3, 27–46, 1966

M. Hough and P. Mayhew, *The British Crime Survey*, HMSO, 1983

R. Kinsey, J. Lea and J. Young, *Losing the Fight*, Blackwell, 1986

R. Kinsey, *The Merseyside Crime Survey*, Merseyside Metropolitan Council, 1984

J. Ditton, *Part-time Crime*, Macmillan, 1979

G. Mars, *Cheats at Work*, Allen Unwin, 1983

PSI Survey *Police and People in London*, The Policy Studies Institute, 1983

S. Holdaway, *Inside the British Police*, Blackwell, 1983

S. Piliavin and S. Briar, *Police Encounters with Juveniles*, American Journal of Sociology, Vol. 52 pp 206–214

D. Sudnow, *Normal Crimes* in P. Worsley, *Problems of Modern Society,* Penguin, 1972

J. Baldwin and M. McConville, *Negotiated Justice*, Martin Robertson, 1977

MRS NEW RIGHT TAKES A LEISURELY STROLL IN THE SUBURBS.

Conservative or 'New Right' Approaches to Crime

In sociology, conservative approaches to crime have largely been ignored. However, they are at present (the late 1980s) the greatest influence on current Home Office policy. Indeed, the influence of all the rest of the theories put together weighs little compared to the conservative one in the current battle against crime.

The conservative tradition is a long one, but as it rarely expressed any clear theoretical explanation for crime and deviance, it does not fit easily into sociological thinking. The approach itself is based upon certain common themes which will be explored shortly, but there are quite distinct schools which have developed from the common ground—in particular, the writings of: (a) Wilson; (b) Van den Haag; and (c) the 'situational prevention' approach of the British Home Office.

The common ground

Consensus

Most conservative thinkers argue that society is based on a common set of values which everybody shares, and the laws derive from these. Laws are therefore a reflection of the will of the people. This idea of consensus in society is a common thread amongst most conservative sociological writers, and underlies their whole approach to the rule of law and the necessity of punishment. The important point here is that from Durkheim onward, the belief that the law reflects the majority consensus in society means to conservatives that those who break the law are acting incorrectly in moral terms. This can be compared to most subcultural, Marxist and labelling approaches which do not see the criminal as necessarily acting immorally. Indeed Marxists actually believe that criminals may be striking a blow for freedom.

The inherent nature of mankind

Human beings are viewed as naturally selfish and self-seeking. However, people are aware that this means there needs to be regulation, and so a framework of laws reflecting the generally accepted morality is instituted. As long as the laws are respected then society can operate. Without obedience to the laws, society would fall into a state of *anomie*.

Rationality

In the conservative model of society, people are assumed to be rational in their actions, making choices and being aware of the consequences. This is the model of 'economic man' who decides whether the benefits of a line of action outweigh the penalties, and then acts accordingly. Exactly the same belief in the essentially rational person is the basis for much right-wing writing in economics, where people operate in a 'market' based on rational responses to supply and demand. Individuals take jobs or leave them, purchase goods or not, on the balance of the benefits to them.

If people really do make economic choices as the conservatives suggest, then they are best left to do so within a society that ensures minimum regulation and maximum 'freedom'. Conservatives disagree with the introduction of laws into areas of personal decision-making, where there is no clear element of morality. For example, the imposition of laws requiring the wearing of seat-belts in cars is wrong (there is no morality here), but laws restricting abortion are necessary and right (reflecting the moral 'consensus' of society).

The concept of rationality is extremely important as it is closely linked to the conservative approach to punishment. The argument is that if people commit crime when the benefits outweigh the costs, then the costs must be increased proportionately over the benefits. This requires heavier, but appropriate punishment and greater policing of the streets to increase the likelihood of being caught.

The role of the government

Although conservatives castigate the State in their writing, it still plays a key part in containing crime. However, they reject the idea that its role is to alter social conditions which liberal and socialist writers claim *cause* crime. Instead they believe that the role of the government is to ensure that people can go about their lawful business (of amassing wealth) with minimum intervention. Furthermore they point, quite correctly, to the fact that during the 1960s when radical measures were taken to alleviate poverty in Britain and America, there was the greatest leap in the number of crimes committed since official recording began. The statistics appear to point to the fact that increases in wealth for the majority of the population are actually linked to an increase in crime, not a decline as most socialist thinkers had traditionally argued.

Some examples of the increase in the crime rate include the fact that for every 100 crimes known to the police in 1939, there were 163 in 1950, 263 in 1960, 550 in 1970, and 891 in 1980. In the ten years between 1971 and 1981, there was a 23 per cent rise in crime in England and Wales.

The table below indicates the rise in crime between 1960 and 1982.

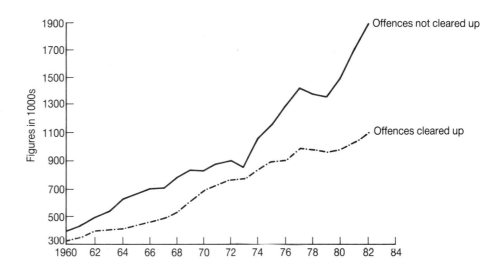

Source: *Criminal Statistics for England and Wales,* reproduced in Kinsey, Lea and Young, *Losing the Fight Against Crime,* Blackwell, 1986

This leads conservatives to the conclusion that the state cannot eliminate crime through tackling its causes, merely by making the costs to the potential criminal outweigh the benefits.

The importance of community

The rule of law is merely a back-up to a far more important form of social control, that of the community. Informal controls imposed by neighbours and fear of 'what others would think' are far stronger in restricting people from committing illegal or anti-social activities than anything the State can do. A central theme in conservative writing from Durkheim onward has been the idea of the *loss of community*. It is only through strengthening the social bonds that constrain people, based on religion, tradition and a sense of belonging (usually to a nation), that crime can be held down to a low level.

The ubiquity of crime

We have just seen that informal controls can help *limit* crime, rather than *eliminate* it. This is because, following Durkheim once again, most conservative writers see the eradication of crime as impossible. This is in contrast to socialist writers, who blame social problems on the capitalist system, and who argue that the elimination of crime will follow the end of the capitalist system. Crime, according to the conservatives will always exist, therefore the aim is to limit its impact.

The importance of order

Conservatives stress above all else the importance of *social order*, that is, the feeling of individuals that they can live without disturbance by others. This may seem obvious and desirable at first, but conservative thinking is that order is more important than strict observance of the law.

Douglas Hurd, the Home Secretary, last night went to the lions' den to debate morality with the church. Speaking at a meeting for General Synod members, he appealed to the Church of England—and to other faiths—to "insist and insist again on the individual standards which are the foundation of a healthy society".

He said: "The nation has pulled itself out of the cycle of defeatism. Confidence has returned ... [but] the most prosperous societies can be impoverished by crime, by violence, and by selfishness. We need to work together to rebuild the moral standards and values which should form the sure foundations of a cohesive and united nation." He was speaking at a meeting which was not part of the official synod business, but took place in the assembly hall, with the Archbishop of Canterbury in the chair. Mr Hurd is the first cabinet minister invited to address a synod gathering in this way.

"I do not agree with those who say that the Church should not comment on social and political problems," said Mr Hurd, but "it follows that the authors of such comment must regard themselves as to some extent having come down from the pulpit. Once they are engaged in political debate, they are on the same mundane level as others who hold strong political views and must be prepared to engage in the ordinary give and take—or even rough and tumble—of practical politics."

Unlike recent Conservative speakers, Mr Hurd did not mention sexual morality. The example he chose was that of violent crime.

The level of violent crime, he said, "has risen at a relentless rate of some 5–7 per cent a year" over the past 30 years, despite "an unrivalled effort to strengthen the police service and toughen the sentences available to the courts".

"We have to influence the behaviour of those who may be tempted into crime," Mr Hurd said. "What society most desperately needs from the churches today is a clear, definite, and repeated statement of personal morality. It often strikes me that many of those who commit violent crime seem genuinely to have no sense whatsoever of the consequences of their actions.

"To them it seems as if the old lady they assault, the young boy whom they abduct, the rival whom they stab, is simply a target, a stuffed doll without any human emotions ...

"The only moral principle to which they respond is the comradeship of the jungle. It is as if, for them, neither the Old nor the New Testament had been written."

Mr Hurd's speech suggests that the Government is giving serious thought to the interplay between morality and the social order, and now expects from the churches a response outside the sphere of sexual morality.

Source: Brown, 'Hurd's moral call to synod', *The Independent,* 11 February, 1988

☐ 1. **According to Hurd, what are the key elements in defeating crime?**
2. **How, if at all, does this fit in with the New Right's position on law and order?**
3. **If you do not agree, which other perspective would you attach it to? Explain your answer.**

Having looked at the common ground of conservative thinking, what I want to do now is to examine the work of two influential writers on crime, Wilson and Van den Haag, and then see how current British policy towards crime is being influenced by conservative thinking.

James Q. Wilson

Wilson has become one of the major influences on law enforcement policy in the United States, although he may be considered a 'maverick' conservative in many ways. For example, unusually for a conservative writer he is opposed to capital punishment. In fact, he places far greater stress on the certainty of capture, rather than the severity of punishment as a deterrent to crime. He does so, because, quite correctly, he points to the very low chances most criminals have of being caught. If the 'economic man' model is true, and people weigh the costs and benefits of crime, then the punishment (the cost) will only be considered if there is a reasonable chance of being caught.

In *Thinking about Crime*, Wilson suggests that eliminating the causes of crime is not possible through government action and he is dismissive of attempts to do so:

> *To people who say 'Crime and drug addiction can only be dealt with by attacking their root causes,' I am sometimes inclined, when in a testy mood, to rejoin: 'stupidity can only be dealt with by attacking its root causes'. I have yet to see a 'root cause' or encounter a government programme that has successfully attacked it . . .*

Wilson goes on to discuss in some detail the work done in the United States during the 1960s to eliminate the causes of poverty, in particular President Johnson's 'War on Want'. Wilson showed that this coincided not with a decline in crime, but a massive increase in it. It is also true that the 1960s saw rapid increases in the rates of crime in Britain too. Furthermore, Wilson points out that there is no direct correlation between the rise in the levels of crime and the levels of unemployment.

As the State cannot eliminate the causes, the role of government is to ensure the cost/benefits of crime are undoubtedly biased in favour of conformity, by increasing the chances of detection.

In order to see how this can be achieved, Wilson and Kelling (in *Broken Windows*) examine the role of the police and conclude that police work can be divided into three kinds: law enforcement; order maintenance; and public service.

Public service consists of such things as traffic control and helping old ladies who are lost. This, according to Wilson, should be handed over to other agencies as it is not a sensible use of police time.

Wilson and Kelling, therefore, turn their attention to the other two aspects of police work. First, they point out that disorder in the streets leads to a breakdown of the social bonds of community. If people are frightened to go out, then the streets become deserted and so petty criminals are free to prey on those who do go out. Eventually law-abiding people move out of the area, leaving it to those too poor to leave and the petty criminals. The result is a huge increase in crime. Therefore, disorder leads to crime, as it weakens the informal social controls of the neighbourhood. Wilson and Kelling suggest that too much attention has been paid by the police to a law enforcement model of policing. A crime is committed, the police are called and attempt to apprehend the culprit, usually without success. Instead, they suggest, the police should be encouraged to engage in policing disorder, even where there has been no crime committed. By this they mean that the police officers 'on the beat' should be encouraged to keep the streets clear of gangs of loitering youths, drunks, etc. It is not that they are necessarily going to commit crime, but that they destroy the social fabric and sense of community in the neighbourhood.

'Public drunkenness, street prostitution, and pornographic displays can destroy a community more quickly than any team of professional burglars'. So they conclude that the police should switch from strict concern with illegal behaviour to containing potential threats to public disorder. This should be seen as a means of upholding and strengthening the sense of community and informal control that prevents crime.

The theory that crime is an expression of the political rage of the dispossessed, rebelling under the iron heel of capitalist tyranny, leaves one wondering why virtually every nation in the world, capitalist, socialist, and communist, has experienced in recent years rapidly increasing crime rates. Such a theory also leaves one dissatisfied with the explanation it purports to offer for why fifteen-year-old boys tear a purse from the hands of a poor black woman on a subway train, or why rioters loot each other's homes but not the bank on the corner.

But above all, I found inexplicable the theories of human nature that seemed to be implicit in much of the public rhetoric about crime. "Men steal because they are poor and deprived." There is more crime in most poor neighborhoods than in most well-off ones, but even in poor communities most people do not steal. Furthermore, crime rose the fastest in this country at a time when the number of persons living in poverty or squalor was declining. No doubt many persons believe that crime produces higher incomes with less effort than available legitimate jobs. But those who are prepared to consider seriously the objective benefits of crime will surely give some, perhaps equal, attention to the objective costs of crime. Therefore, it cannot be simply the case that "men steal because they are poor." If objective conditions are used to explain crime, then the full statement must be: "Men steal because the benefits of stealing exceed the costs of stealing by a wider margin than the benefits of working exceed the costs of working." In short, spokesmen who use poverty as an explanation of crime should, by the force of their own logic, be prepared to consider the capacity of society to deter crime by raising the risks of crime. But they rarely do. Indeed, those who use poverty as an explanation are largely among the ranks of those who vehemently deny that crime can be deterred.

Advocates of increasing the harshness of penalties commit the same error, but in the opposite direction. "Man will not steal if the penalty is sufficiently severe." No doubt, very severe penalties will deter many people from stealing, *if* those who consider stealing believe the penalty is likely to be exacted; *if* the penalty, discounted by the chances of avoiding it, is of greater value than the proceeds of the crime, discounted by the chances of not getting away with it; and *if* there is another source of income (such as a job) that would produce greater net gains. The United States has, on the whole, the most severe set of criminal penalties in its lawbooks of any advanced Western nation; it also has the highest crime rate of most advanced Western nations.

Throughout I use the word "crime" as if we all knew what this meant. Of course we do not. It is a term that covers everything from white-collar bank embezzlement to blue-collar rape. Rather than burden the reader with countless distinctions and categories, I have instead adopted a simplifying rule: Unless otherwise stated or clearly implied, the word "crime" when used alone in this book refers to predatory crime for gain, the most common forms of which are robbery, burglary, larceny, and auto theft.

This book deals neither with "white-collar crimes" nor, except for heroin addiction, with so-called "victimless crimes." Partly this reflects the limits of my own knowledge, but it also reflects my conviction, which I believe is the conviction of most citizens, that predatory street crime is a far more serious matter than consumer fraud, antitrust violations, prostitution, or gambling, because predatory crime makes difficult or impossible the maintenance of meaningful human communities. Even those who agree with the greater importance of street crime may nonetheless argue that police preoccupation with "victimless crimes" seriously impedes their attention to more serious matters. I disagree. Though millions of persons are arrested each year for drunkenness, prostitution, and marijuana possession, and though one can raise grave questions about the propriety of arrest as a response to these behaviors, in fact, the police devote very few resources to these matters (for example, drunk arrests are as easy as traffic arrests and require only a few officers, or a little time from each officer, to produce large numbers). Furthermore, what is listed as a "drunk" arrest or a "marijuana" arrest is typically an arrest for another reason (disorderly conduct, a traffic violation) in which the presence of alcohol or marijuana leads to the imposition of more serious charges.

Source: Wilson, *Thinking about Crime,* Basic Books, 1975

☐ 1. **What are the key elements of the 'New Right' position on crime? Construct a chart and fit the arguments presented in this extract and in the main text in the appropriate columns.**

2. **What are victimless crimes? Why do liberal commentators regard them as unimportant? Why, do you think, does Wilson regard them as very important indeed?**

3. **How would Marxists criticise this approach?**

4. **Is there any way to prove/disprove Wilson's assertion that 'crime rose the fastest in this country (the USA) at a time when the number of persons living in poverty or squalor was declining?'**

Van den Haag

In *Punishing Criminals*, Van den Haag argues that inequality is inherent in the capitalist system, as the whole basis of the system is to reward people according to the risks they are taking and the abilities they have to offer. Of course, Van den Haag believes that this is a good thing to be preserved. However, inherent in this system is the temptation for the losers in the race for wealth to 'cheat' and try to deprive the affluent of what they have obtained, or to overturn the entire economic system. Therefore, laws are needed which will restrain them from doing so.

Van den Haag argues that those who believe the law generally imposes itself on the poor rather than the rich and who claim that this is a sign of unfairness, are completely mistaken. It is obvious, he points out, that the law is going to deal mainly with the poor, because there is little reason why the more successful should commit crime. The entire purpose of the law is and *should be* to prevent the poorer sections of the community from taking from the affluent or trying to bring about revolutionary changes.

The basis of the law is coercion against the poor and this is absolutely necessary. It is not, however, that the law is unfair or applied unequally, it is merely that those who are most likely to break the law come from the poorer sections of society. There is little interest in white-collar or corporate crime in Van den Haag's writings.

Van den Haag's explanation for law-breaking is therefore based on an awareness that crime is the inevitable outcome of capitalist society. However, it can be limited (apart from through punishment) by strict emphasis on moral rules and family discipline.

On social policy, Van den Haag argues for a strengthening of moral codes and a penal code based on proportional punishment for the crime which also takes into account the position in society of the transgressor. Perhaps an example will make this clear. If a police officer and an unemployed man commit a burglary, strictly speaking they have both committed the same offence and, therefore, ought to be punished equally. However, conservative notions of justice (which pervade our judicial system) argue that the police officer must be punished more severely because of his/her position in society. So, it is not just the offence that is important but who commits the offence.

The main aim of the law is *deterrence* and, therefore, publicity is important in order to point out to others what happens when the limits of acceptable behaviour are breached. There are clearly links to Durkheim. The principal of deterrence is the reason why so many conservatives are in favour of capital punishment.

Milton Friedman

Friedman is an economist rather than a criminologist, but he has commented on crime, in relation to the general philosophy of 'market liberalism'. As his ideas differ in emphasis from Wilson and Van den Haag, it is worth giving them a brief examination.

In *Free to Choose*, Friedman discusses the impact of the 'drive to equality' which he claims marks the policies of various post-war governments before Mrs Thatcher's. According to him, most people do not believe in the movement towards greater equality. The result has been that most people have evaded the law, for example by tax evasion. Lack of respect for laws is infectious in that once people see others breaking the law and 'getting away with it', they ask themselves why should they continue to respect the law. Again, once one set of laws are treated with disdain, disrespect for other laws increases; even those laws which people generally believe are right and proper—such as laws against vandalism, theft and violence. The end result is that crime becomes widespread. Friedman concludes, 'hard as it may be to believe, the growth of crude criminality in Britain in recent decades may well be one consequence of the drive for equality.'

Why does Friedman see equality as such an evil thing? The answer goes back to our discussion earlier on *freedom*. Freedom and equality are incompatible, for any government's attempt to eliminate extremes of poverty and wealth must, by its very nature, infringe the 'liberty' of the citizens by imposing the will of the State on them. Furthermore, equality eliminates the incentive required to create a dynamic wealth-producing nation and this is one of the major reasons for Britain's economic decline since the 1940s, according to Friedman.

Friedman, following the writings of Hayek, (probably the most important New Right thinker of all), sees the welfare state as the primary cause of the problems faced by society, and crime rates could be brought down by *reducing* welfare provision. This runs against most other liberal and left arguments that dominate sociology. Friedman, and the most of the New Right, argue that the growth of 'Welfare-ism' has undermined the social bonds that hold society together. The primary units of family and community have become redundant as the welfare state has provided an 'easy option' for those who do not want to meet their social obligations. As the State will take over when problems arise, it is no longer necessary for family members to provide care for the old. As the family is seen as the very basis of society, its undermining pulls down the entire structure. A relevant example is the way that everybody 'minds their own business', and what goes on in the street outside is nothing to do with them. This is a licence for criminals to operate. On top of this people see it as the role of the police to control crime, failing to see that it is a general social obligation. The message is not to look for others to provide solutions to social problems. As Mrs Thatcher puts it, a healthy society is one where 'people . . . care for others and look first to themselves to care for themselves' (*Let our Children Grow Tall*).

Criticisms

The conservative approach has come in for a number of criticisms, particularly, and fairly predictably, from the Left. These criticisms derive from the fundamentally different assumptions of the Left. They argue, that the conservative approach is merely a justification for keeping people unequal. Some conservatives would agree on this and would then justify inequality from their perspective. This is less a debate over the rights or wrongs of the conservative viewpoint and more a debate over morality. This is also true of the conservatives' belief in the natural greed of individuals. Marxists argue that this greed exists because of the way capitalism socialises people. There does appear

☐ **What parallels, if any, can be drawn between the New Right and anomie? Construct a diagram comparing the two approaches, using such headings as 'the law', 'reasons why people commit crime', 'ways of preventing crime', etc.**
What policy proposals emerge? How do these differ from the policy proposals of the neo-Marxists and labelling theorists?

to be a massive contradiction in the conservative position, however, in that conservatives elevate the search for success to a central moral value of capitalism, stressing the need to compete and look after oneself rather than others. However, on the other hand, they lament the lack of community and the selfish way people behave. Community and self-seeking greed seem opposites rather than the complementary values (as the conservatives see them). A further criticism is that if financial gain is promoted as a morally praiseworthy goal, it can't be too surprising that people try to achieve it through any way open to them, such as 'crime'. Merton saw this contradiction in his discussion of anomie almost fifty years ago, yet the lesson appears to be ignored by conservatives today.

Social policy towards crime in Britain today

The liberal approach

Current policy in Britain represents a partial victory for the New Right. This is reflected in the change in direction of policing in recent years and in the current output of the Home Office Research Unit. The New Right has won because the liberal reforms of the 1960s in the United States and, to a lesser extent, Britain, have clearly failed to halt the increase in crimes. In fact, it was during the very real attempts in the 1960s to combat poverty, to introduce educational reforms, and to extend welfare services that the largest increases of crime took place. These liberal reforms had been partially influenced by subcultural theory, particularly that of Cloward and Ohlin (see p. 34), as well as an interpretation of Merton's anomie theory. In essence, it was argued that by giving society's poorer sections a way to succeed through better education, welfare and social security benefits, they would be removed from the economic temptations and the criminal-encouraging values of their subcultures. Unfortunately, this did not work.

The Marxists

'Piecemeal social engineering' as it was called, was attacked by both the extreme Left and the extreme Right. The Marxists saw it as fundamentally flawed as it did not tackle the *structural* causes of crime, by which they meant the economic and social structure of capitalism.

Their solution was to call for a fundamental restructuring of society along socialist lines. This has little appeal for the electorate and, therefore, was generally ignored. The trouble with Marxist-based approaches to social policy are that they are so radical that they have little chance of ever being used in Britain.

The New Right

The extreme Right attacked the liberal social engineering, believing it helped to *increase* crime by undermining the value of individual responsibility, which in turn weakened social integration, so that people were less restrained. Their solution was to abandon the welfare state and introduce sweeping economic 'reforms', which place great stress on individuals looking after themselves. They believe individual responsibility within an openly competitive economic framework, and backed by effective policing, would restore crime levels to a low level once again.

It is this model, considerably modified under Home Office pressure, plus political 'reality' (cutting down too obviously on the welfare state would be political suicide) which has been the most influential. Its underlying assumptions have been taken on board in the 'battle against crime'. The result is what is known as *administrative criminology* or the *multi-agency model.*

Administrative criminology

In Britain, the conservative approach has partially merged with the *multi-causal* approach we examined on pages 40 and 85. The outcome has been the work of writers such as Clarke and Hough. They point out that as the causes of crime are so complex, relating to a number of factors such as family socialisation, peer group influence at school, in work and in the neighbourhood, it is beyond the resources of the State to eliminate them. On the other hand, they show quite clearly (see *Crime and Police Effectiveness*) that increasing police numbers does not result in increased chances of apprehending criminals (as Wilson and Van den Haag believe it would). Given this, the Home Office has effectively abondoned any interest in tackling the causes of crime, and has swung all its resources to preventing crime occurring, without demanding too great an increase in police officers.

Lea and Young have used the term *administrative criminology* to explain this approach mainly because it stresses that crime can be tackled through a series of administrative measures which make the sheer fact of committing a crime more difficult.

[This has . . .] become the official policy on crime in the last few years. It is called crime prevention, and it is to be achieved by the 'multi-agency approach'.

It began with a seminar at Bramshill [Police College] in 1982 convened by Home Office official Sir Brian Cubbon, backed up by an official circular to police, schools, social services, housing departments and others. A variant of it—what Vivien Stern, the director of the National Association for the Care and Resettlement of Offenders, calls 'locks and things'— was the theme of the Prime Minister's seminars on crime prevention; if you lock everything up, it can't get stolen, ergo no more theft.

'It is now accepted that the impact of the criminal justice system on the actual level of offending is low; its role is essentially symbolic' writes Stephen Shaw, director of the Prison Reform Trust in *Crime UK*, one of the Policy Journals series. He is saying what other criminologists have said: that the criminal justice system is 'rhetorical', more to do with a public discourse on law and order than effective measures on crime. When Tory ministers rise at Tory Party conferences to announce with a flourish the latest deterrent—short sharp shocks, minimum life-sentences—most of those trying to make the system work are merely cynical.

The multi-agency approach is a tacit official recognition that the causes of crime are social, though these will range from the social 'culture of permissiveness' amongst parents and teachers favoured by the right, to mass unemployment, crummy housing and a general loss of hope favoured by the left. It also involved using victim surveys, begun in the USA in the 1960s and increasingly popular in Britain in the 1980s, to find out where most crime is committed and who is most affected. Crime Prevention strategies can then be targeted. A special police Crime Prevention Unit has been set up the Home Office to monitor and advise on such strategies.

The discovery that the main victims of crime are the poor has made this a popular new starting point in urban regeneration.

Source: Benton, 'The Absence of Acceptable Authority', *The New Statesman*, 14 November, 1986

☐ 1. What does the author mean by saying that the 'criminal justice system is "rhetorical"'?

2. What sort of 'remedies' does the multi-agency approach favour for dealing with crime?

3. What does it view as the 'causes'?

4. Do these two answers appear to 'match' according to you? Explain your answer.

5. Does the multi-agency approach fit the policies of the 'Left' or the 'Right'?

There are a number of measures which have been taken.

Styles of policing

The debate over foot patrol versus car patrol has largely been won by those in favour of police officers going out on foot. The only policing justifications for most police officers to travel around in cars are in response to emergencies and for traffic patrol. However, police officers are extremely reluctant to give up their cars as they provide them with shelter and somewhere to rest comfortably. Long walks on 'beats' in all weathers contradicts the self-image of a 'profession', which has been assiduously cultivated by police officers. This opposition has slowed down any significant move towards foot patrol.

Types of policing

There are two 'ideal types' of policing: consensus and military, as shown in the diagram below:

Subject	Consensus policing	Military policing
The public	supports the police	fears/is in conflict with the police
Information from the public	large amount, relevant to crime detection and specific	small amount, low-grade and general
Mode of gathering information	public-initiated, low use of police surveillance technology	police-initiated, extensive use of surveillance technology
Police profile	low profile, integrated with community, police officers as citizens	high profile, police as outsiders, marginalised, use of force and special militarised units
Targeting by police	of specific offenders	of social groups/ stereotyped populations
Style of police intervention	individual, consensual, reactive	generalised, coercive, proactive
Ideal typical example	English village	Northern Ireland

Source: Kinsey, Lea and Young, *Losing the Fight against Crime,* Blackwell, 1986

At present the two types are being used in different areas for policing different 'populations'. Areas targetted as 'high risk' by the police are controlled by military policing. Usually these are inner city areas, typically with high proportions of black people. Suburbs and rural areas are treated to consensus policing.

☐ PROJECT

1 To find out more about 'preventive crime', obtain a copy of *Practical Ways to Crack Crime,* HMSO 1988, and examine the 'solutions' it proposes to crime. The Neighbourhood Watch Scheme is particularly interesting. Find out what it is. Find a local Neighbourhood Watch Scheme (ask the police) and arrange an interview with the local 'co-ordinator' and assess how effective he/she thinks it has been. Can you uncover any statistics to check on the replies?

Assess the social class of the areas—is anything noticeable?

Critics of Neighbourhood Watch argue that they simply have a spillover effect, so that crime moves elsewhere but does not diminish. Interview the police to assess their view of this argument.

Secondly, critics argue that Neighbourhood Watch schemes are simply groups of middle class families banding together to protect their property.

Assess the social class of Neighbourhood Watch schemes in your town. The best way to do this is by using the houses as a guide to social class.

2 The concepts of 'informal controls' and 'community' are extremely hard to measure. However, devise a questionnaire/experiment/method of observation which gives you a guide to the extent to which social controls operate in an area.

You could, for example, interview local people to find out where they thought the boundaries of their own 'neighbourhood' were. Ask them what they would do in a series of hypothetical situations (suspicious character next door, noisy youths in the street etc.) You would have to be careful to obtain a range of ages etc. Does a community with strong 'informal controls' exist?

Police in confrontation with striking P&O dockers, 1988.

Situational prevention

This involves making it more difficult for criminals to steal. In practice, the police encourage householders to take precautions against theft, for example fitting locks on windows, installing burglar alarms and marking property with postal codes. It is now extending to the design of articles. For instance, vandal-proof phone boxes are replacing the old red ones, and car manufacturers are trying to build mechanisms into cars to prevent theft and vandalism.

Neighbourhood Watch schemes

These involve encouraging people in certain areas to be 'good neighbours' and keep an eye on each others' houses. At the sign of any possible intruder they should contact the police. The Neighbourhood Watch schemes have tended to succeed more in middle class than working class areas. In some inner city areas, grants are being provided to enable community committees to be set up, without any clear link to crime prevention being mentioned.

The common thread running through these approaches is the belief, dear to the conservatives, that if only a sense of community can be recreated then crime can be held down.

☐ **ESSAYS**

1 **The New-Right are currently the most influential voice in policy making in Britain. Critically discuss the arguments they put forward.**
2 **Compare the approach of the New-Right with those of the Marxists and labelling theorists. What differences in policy towards crime would they suggest?**

Bibliography

J. Q. Wilson, *Thinking About Crime*, Random House, 1977

Van den Haag, *Punishing Criminals*, Basic books, 1975

J. Wilson and G. Kelling, *Broken Windows*, Atlantic Monthly, pp 29–38, March 1982

M. Friedman, *Free to Choose*, Avon, 1980

R. Clarke and M. Hough, *Crime and Police Effectiveness*, HMSO, 1984

General Bibliography

Becker, H. *The Outsiders*, The Free Press, 1963

Box, S. *Deviance, Reality and Society,* 2nd ed. Holt Saunders, 1981

Box, S. *Power, Crime and Mystification,* Tavistock, 1983

Centre for Contemporary Cultural Studies, *The Empire Strikes Back,* Hutchinson, 1982

Chambliss, W. S. and Mankoff, M. (eds) *Whose Law? What Order?,* Wiley, 1976

Cohen, A. *Delinquent Boys, the Culture of the Gang,* The Free Press, 1955

Cloward, R. and Ohlin, L., *Delinquency and Opportunity,* The Free Press, 1961

Downes, D. *The Delinquent Solution,* RKP, 1966

Hall, S. and Jefferson, T. (eds) *Resistance Through Rituals,* Hutchinson, 1976

Heidensohn, F. *Women and Crime,* Macmillan, 1985

Holdaway, S. *Inside the British Police,* Blackwell, 1983

Hough, M. and Mayhew, P. *Taking Account of Crime,* HMSO, 1985

Kinsey, R., Lea, J. and Young, J. *Losing the Fight Against Crime,* Blackwell, 1986

Lea, J. and Young, J. *What is to be done about law and order?,* Penguin, 1984

Matza, D. *Delinquency and Drift,* Wiley, 1964

Parker H. *A View from the Boys,* David and Charles, 1974

Pearce, F. *Crimes of the Powerful,* Pluto, 1976

Taylor, I. *et al, The New Criminology,* RKP, 1973

West, D. J. and Farrington, D. P. *The Delinquent Way of Life,* Heinemann, 1977

Author Index

Subject Index

Acknowledgements

The author and publisher are indebted to the following:
For permission to reproduce text extracts and diagrams;

Basil Blackwell for material from *Folk Devils and Moral Panics*, S. Cohen, 1980;
Blackwell for material from *Losing The Fight Against Crime*, Kinsey, Lea and Young, 1986;
and for material from *Girl Delinquents,* Campbell, 1981;
Collins Publishers for the extract from *The Politics of the Judician* by J A Griffith;
The Guardian for extracts from the articles 'Sombre "Rehearsal" led to Boy's Death' (March 1983); 'A Painful Probe for Two Drug Groups' and 'Ban on Pig Drug Lifted by EEC' (June 1987); 'Trials and Errors' (February 1987);
Gower Publishing Company Limited for material from *British Social Attitudes* by R Jowell and S Witherspoon, 1985;
Harper and Row Ltd for the extract from *Thinking About Crime* by J Wilson;
The Controller of Her Majesty's Stationery Office for extracts from *The Trend of the Relationship Between Crime and Unemployment During the Period 1950–1980* and the diagram from *Race, Crimes and Arrests* by Stevens and Willis, 1979;
The Independent for the article 'Rise in crime rate of 1% is lowest for at least 30 years' (March 1988); and the extract from 'Hurd's Moral Call to Synod' (February 1988);
Macmillan Publishing Company for the extract from *Outsiders: Studies in the Sociology of Deviance* by Howard Becker, 1963; and material from *Violence Against Wives* by Dobash and Dobash, 1979;
The New Statesman for the extract from 'The Absence of Acceptable Authority' by S Benton (November 1986); and 'The Great Greed' by D Bouchier (June 1987);
New Society for the extract from 'Jobless turn to Crime, study shows' (November 1986); and the extract from 'Crime, Police and People' (January 1986);
The Open University Press for the material from *Crime and Punishment* by Bottomley and Pease, 1986;
The Observer for material from 'Racism's Short Fuse' (November 1987); and 'The Quality of Mercy' (July 1987);
Routledge and Kegan Paul for an extract from *Marital Violence and Public Policy* by J Pahl, 1985;
Stanley Thornes for a diagram from *'Sociology Alive!'* by S Moore, 1987;
The Times Higher Educational Supplement for an extract from a review by Banton on 'Police and People in London' (January 1984) and an extract from 'Keeping the Force in Check' by Banton (January 1984);
The Women's Press for figures from *Sexual Violence: the reality for Women,* 1984.

While every effort has been made to contact copyright-holders, this has not proved possible in every case. The publishers would be pleased to hear from any copyright-holders not acknowledged.

For permission to reproduce illustrations;

Format (Pam Isherwood) p. 10, p. 70
Associated Press Limited, p. 25
Barnaby's Picture Library (D. Ridgers) p. 38
Daily Express, p. 70
David Parkins, p. 71
Angela Martin, p. 103
Christine Roche, p. 108
The Press Association, p. 154